Simple
Scrapbooks

digital designs
for scrapbooking 2

making your own

BY RENEE PEARSON

contents

welcome to **digital designs for scrapbooking 2**,
scrapbooking—it's not just for paper anymore!

Digital scrapbooking is rapidly setting the standard for creative, beautiful, professional-looking pages. With the sky-rocketing proliferation of digital cameras and high-quality photo printers, scrapbookers everywhere are taking their scrapbooking projects to whole new levels in the digital world.

As a designer and illustrator, I realized early on that the digital realm was the perfect environment for my scrapbooking projects. And I'm not alone—thousands of scrapbookers feel the same way. But resources for digital scrapbookers, while growing, are still limited. That's why I teach classes, write for two popular magazines, and—more importantly—why I wrote my first book, *Digital Designs for Scrapbooking*. In that book, I showed scrapbookers how to create easy, beautiful layouts from templates and from "scratch."

As it turned out, that's exactly what scrapbookers wanted to learn! That book was such a success that readers asked for more—a lot more! So *Digital Designs for Scrapbooking 2: Making Your Own* was born.

In *Digital Designs for Scrapbooking 2: Making Your Own*, it's your turn to unleash your creativity and design your own elements to make striking scrapbook layouts. In it, I'll show you how to create the building blocks that make up a beautiful digital scrapbook page:

- Backgrounds using patterns, type, the distressed look, and more

- Embellishments such as brads, tags, bookplates, and chipboard letters and shapes
- Stamps, frames, and edge effects, using tools like brushes and masks

Each lesson in this book is simple, practical, and fun. When you're finished with the easy-to-follow steps in an exercise, you'll have created something you can use right away in your scrapbooking projects.

WHAT YOU NEED TO KNOW

In this book, I assume you are at least somewhat familiar with Adobe Photoshop Elements' basic concepts and techniques for working with layers, tools, and their options.

If you're not familiar with Photoshop Elements, you may want to explore Photoshop Elements **Help** before you tackle the steps in this book. However, you don't have to be an expert—I promise to guide you through each project step-by-step, and you'll learn more about the features in Photoshop Elements as you complete each easy-to-follow exercise.

The exercises in each chapter are designed to be used with Adobe Photoshop Elements 5.0 or 4.0 on a PC or 4.0 on a Mac. The screenshots that illustrate each exercise were taken using a PC and Adobe Photoshop Elements 5.0. You may see minor differences if you're using Photoshop Elements 4.0.

The first three chapters of this book contain lessons and exercises that will show you how to create the ingredients for a gorgeous layout. The fourth chapter, called "Remind Me!" is a quick reference to the major tasks from the lessons—if you need a quick refresher on how to define a brush or how to add a metallic finish to an element, for example, you'll find it in that chapter.

At the end of the book, you'll find the Gallery. I asked some of my favorite digital designers to use the techniques from this book to design their own digital scrapbook layouts. I know you'll enjoy the amazing array of pages these digital divas created. They are truly works of art, just like your own pages will be!

ⓓ DESIGN TIP

In this book, you'll use a single color palette, called *Lolly*, for all the exercises. This ensures that all your creations will match each other, and the *Lolly* kit included on this book's CD.

ⓣ TECH TIP

For the steps in this book, I'll show you the menu option for each command. As you become more familiar with Photoshop Elements, you may find that you prefer using keyboard shortcuts for the tasks you perform most often. For example, instead of using the **Edit** menu to select **Copy**, you can press the **CTRL** and **C** keys.

When keyboard shortcuts are available for a task, you'll find the shortcut listed next to the menu command. You'll be surprised at how quickly you'll memorize them and what a difference they'll make in speeding up your work!

WHAT'S ON THE CD?

Don't forget to check out the CD that comes with this book—it's chock-full of goodies you can use as you design your own scrapbook page elements:

- The *Lolly* set—a complete digital kit of backgrounds and elements (I designed it especially for this book!)
- The *Lolly* color palette so you can create your own color coordinated backgrounds and elements to match the kit
- Templates for digital elements
- Extras, such as brushes and overlays
- A printable .pdf that shows you all the goodies we've included, along with their file names.

READY, SET, DESIGN!

Digital Designs for Scrapbooking 2 has everything you need to get started building your own stash of digital scrapbooking ingredients. How you mix and stir and blend those ingredients is up to you and your creative muse. I know with this book in one hand and your mouse in the other, you'll find wonderful, beautiful, easy ways to turn all those photographic memories into the works of art they deserve to be. It's that Simple.

Renee

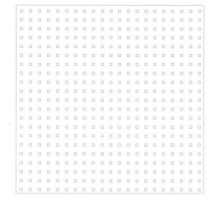
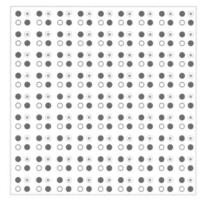

creating backgrounds

Every great page layout begins with a great background. So it follows that the best place to begin creating your own digital elements is with backgrounds. In this chapter, we'll look at three different ways to create backgrounds using Adobe Photoshop Elements:

- Repeating shapes to create an all-over pattern
- Using typed words and letters to make
  a background with real impact
- Layering images from several files to create
  a distressed look

For the exercises in this chapter, you'll use the Lolly color swatch, and you'll create a variety of 8 x 8 color-coordinated background pages you will be proud to use in your own projects.

create coordinated backgrounds using patterns

One of the easiest ways to make backgrounds for your scrapbook pages is to create simple patterns and then repeat them across the page. Adobe Photoshop Elements makes it easy to design, save, and use patterns.

 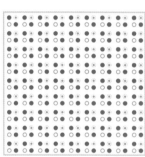

In this exercise, I'll show you how to design two simple, geographic patterns from shapes that are standard in Photoshop Elements. Then you'll use different colors to make several stunning backgrounds from those two designs.

At the end of this exercise, you'll have created a single master Photoshop PSD (.psd) file with lots of layers in it—you'll be able to combine the different layers into many different individual backgrounds, each of which you'll save as a separate JPEG (.jpg) file. That will give you a variety of backgrounds to use as you create your scrapbooking projects.

CREATING THE FIRST PATTERN

Follow these steps to create the first patterned background.

STEP 1: Open Photoshop Elements and go to the Editor workspace.

If this is the first time you've used Photoshop Elements, a welcome screen appears. From the welcome screen select **Edit and Enhance Photos**. ❶ If the welcome screen doesn't appear, make sure you are in the Editor workspace. (If you aren't, click the **Edit** icon, then click **Go to Full Edit**.)

If the Photo Bin at the bottom of the screen is open, you can close or shrink it. You won't need it in this exercise.

STEP 2: Open a new blank file by opening the **File** menu and clicking **Blank File**. In the **Name** box, type *digipatterns*. Set the **Width** to 2" and the **Height** to 2". Set the **Resolution** to 300 pixels/inch, the **Color Mode** to RGB Color, and the **Background Contents** to White. ❷ Then click **OK**.

STEP 3: So you can see the dimensions of your document, open the **View** menu and click **Rulers**.

STEP 4: To display a grid to help you line up the elements on your page, open the **View** menu and click **Grid**. Then from the **View** menu, point to **Snap to**. If Grid isn't checked, choose **Grid** so elements will snap into place on the gridlines, lining them up more evenly. Then set the grid to ⅛" markings by opening the **Edit** menu, pointing to **Preferences**, then clicking **Grid**. Set Subdivisions to 8 and click **OK**.

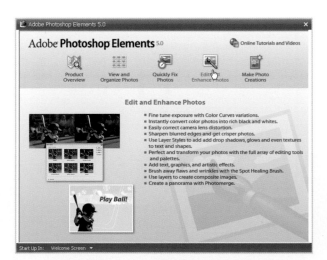

❶ The Photoshop Elements Welcome screen.

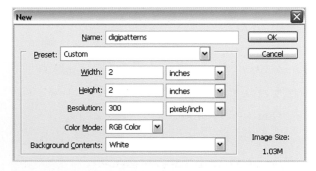

❷ Settings for the new blank file.

TECH TIP

You can turn the grid off and on as often as you wish. Choosing **Grid** from the **View** menu toggles the grid on and off. You can also toggle the rulers on and off.

STEP 5: To create the first pattern, you'll use shapes from Photoshop Elements' Custom Shape picker. First, select the **Custom Shape** tool 🗩 from the toolbox along the left side of the screen. This changes the options in the bar at the top of the screen to show some common shapes.

More shapes are available in the **Custom Shape Picker**. To open the **Custom Shape Picker**, click the **Shape** drop-down list.

Now click the arrow button in the top right corner of the **Custom Shape Picker** and choose **Shapes** from the list of shape collections that appears. ❸

STEP 6: Select the **Rounded Square Frame** shape. (To see the name of each shape, hover the cursor over it.)

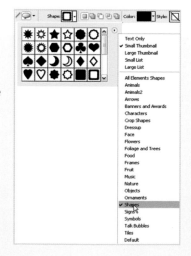

❸ Select **Shapes** from the **Custom Shape Picker** list of collections.

STEP 7: Starting anywhere in the window, click and drag to draw a ⅛" shape. Just make sure you leave at least ⅛" of white space around the shape. ❹

Notice that a new layer, called *Shape 1*, is added to the **Layers** palette. ❺

TECH TIP

Each item on the page has its own layer. Some layers, like the background layer, cover the entire page. Others appear to cover only a portion of the page, but actually they have some filled pixels (the ones you see) and some transparent pixels (the ones you don't see).

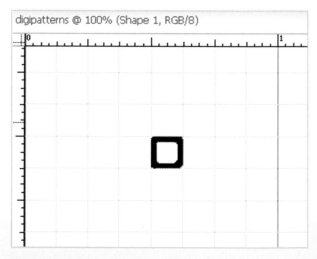

❹ Draw a ⅛" shape, leaving at least ⅛" of white space around the shape.

❺ The *Shape 1* layer is added to the **Layers** palette.

Each pane of glass has something painted on it. When you stack them, you can see the entire composition through the clear areas. Each layer in Photoshop Elements is like one pane of glass, and the clear areas are the transparent pixels. The bottom layer is the bottom pane of glass. To make something on one piece of glass appear on top of another piece of glass, you movie it up in the stack.

In Photoshop Elements, if you don't want one layer to show at all, you can turn off its visibility by clicking its eye icon in the **Layers** palette. You don't have to remove the layer from the stack of layers, like you would if it were glass. That way you can turn the layer on and off to change your document's look.

STEP 8: Before you change the shape's color, you need to replace the default color swatches in Photoshop Elements with the color swatches on the CD that came with this book. In the options

❻ The Lolly color swatches.

❶ **INFO TIP**
The **Color Swatches** palette is a convenient place to store frequently used colors. You can add colors to the default swatches or replace them with other palettes.

bar, click the **Color** drop-down list. Click **Options**, then click **Load Color Swatches**. Browse to the CD and locate the file *lolly.aco*. Then click **Load**. The Lolly color swatches are now ready to use. ❻

STEP 9: To change the shape's color, click **lime** in the color swatch. (Hover the cursor over each color to see its name.)

STEP 10: This shape, plus a small amount of white space around it to allow for proper spacing, is the pattern we want to repeat across the entire document. To do that, you'll identify a portion of this image as a "pattern." First, select the **Rectangular Marquee tool** ⌞¯⌝ from the toolbox. Click and drag the selection marquee to select the area around the shape ⅜" in size. ❼

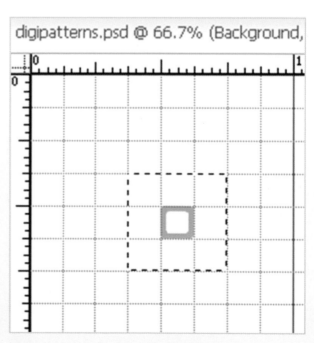

❼ The area you want to define as the pattern is selected.

STEP 11: Turn off the background layer's visibility by clicking its eye icon in the **Layers** palette. This will make your new pattern have a transparent background. **8**

STEP 12: Now you can define the pattern. First, select the *Background* layer by clicking its layer name in the **Layers** palette. Next, from the **Edit** menu, choose **Define Pattern from Selection**. Name the pattern *digipattern1* and click **OK**.

ℹ INFO TIP

Photoshop Elements won't create a pattern if a shape layer is selected. Therefore, you simply have to select a non-shape layer. It doesn't even matter that the layer's visibility is turned off. The pattern will be defined by all the layers that are currently visible.

If you only have one layer in your pattern file, and it's a shape layer, you'll need to **Simplify** the layer before defining it as a pattern. To do that, make sure the layer is selected, then click

the **More** button at the top of the **Layers** palette and choose **Simplify Layer**.

Now this pattern has been saved and you can use it later to create backgrounds for scrapbook pages.

First, however, let's create a second pattern to use.

ⅾ DESIGN TIP

For this exercise, you used a 2 x 2 document to create your initial pattern, because the pattern itself will be small and simple. You will create a larger page that uses the repeating pattern to make several fun backgrounds. When you're designing your own patterns from scratch and you're not sure what the finished size will be, simply select a file size larger than you think you'll need for the pattern.

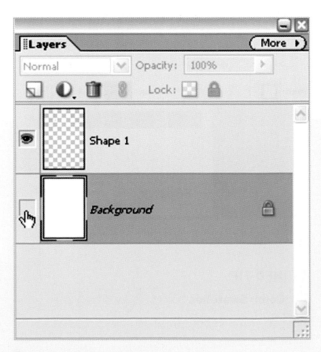

8 To turn off the background layer's visibility, click the eye icon.

CREATING THE SECOND PATTERN

You will create a second pattern in this same file, just so everything is handy in a single file. Because the first pattern has been defined already, and we won't be using that shape in the next pattern we define, that shape layer isn't important anymore (at least for now). You can delete it if you want, or you could open a new file and start from the beginning again. However, I like to keep all the layers in a single document unless it gets too confusing. That way, all my layers are available if I need them, and I can just turn visibility on and off as necessary.

To create the second pattern, keep using the same file, and follow these steps.

STEP 1: Since we won't be using the first shape, turn off the *Shape 1* layer's visibility by clicking its eye icon in the **Layers** palette, and turn on visibility of the white *Background* layer. Then select the *Shape 1* layer. That way, when we create a new shape layer, it will be created above the *Shape 1* layer.

ⓣ TECH TIP
You can drag layers up and down in the **Layers** palette, so if a layer gets created in an unexpected place, just move it to its proper position.

STEP 2: Select the **Custom Shape** tool from the toolbox. In the options bar, open the **Custom Shape Picker** and select the filled **Circle** shape.

STEP 3: Begin ¼" from the top of the document and ⅛" from the left edge of the document, and click and drag to draw the shape ¼" in diameter. Notice that a new layer has been added to the **Layers** palette.

STEP 4: To change the shape's color, click the **Color** box to open the color swatches, and then click **turquoise**. ❶

STEP 5: Draw another ¼" circle beginning ⅛" to the right of the first circle. Change its color to *lime*. ❷

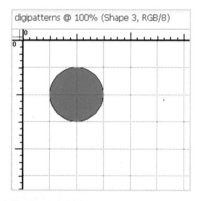

❶ Change the shape's color to turquoise

❷ Change the second circle's color to lime.

STEP 6: To reduce this shape to half its original size, from the **Image** menu, point to **Transform Shape**, then click **Free Transform Shape**. In the options bar, click **Constrain Proportions**, then change either the width or height to 50% and press **ENTER**. The shape will be reduced to half its size. Press **ENTER** again to commit to the change (or you can click the **checkmark** to commit). ❸

STEP 7: Open the **Custom Shape Picker** again and choose the **Circle Thin Frame** shape. Draw a ¼" circle around the smaller lime circle. Change this new circle's color to **tangerine**. ❹

STEP 8: From the **Custom Shape Picker** choose the **Circle Frame** shape. Draw a ¼" circle ⅛" below the first turquoise circle, and change the new circle's color to lime. ❺

STEP 9: The last shape is a repeat of the first. You could redraw it, but instead let's duplicate the first shape and move it into place. Select the *Shape 2* layer in the **Layers** palette. From the **Layer** menu, click **Duplicate Layer**. Accept the default name (*Shape 2 copy*) and click **OK**. The new copy will be on top of the old shape, so you won't be able to see the old one. Don't worry, it's there.

To keep your layers in the same order you drew them, drag this layer to the top of the **Layers** palette. ❻

Select the **Move** tool from the toolbox, click inside the document window, then drag your new copy of the turquoise circle ⅛" below the lime and tangerine circles, and ⅛" to the right of the lime circle. ❼

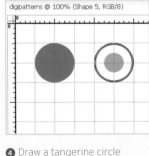

❹ Draw a tangerine circle around the lime circle.

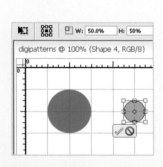

❸ After reducing the circle's size, click the **checkmark** or press **ENTER** to commit to the change.

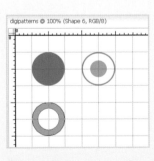

❺ Draw a lime circle beneath the first circle.

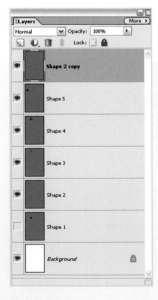

❻ Drag the new layer to the top of the **Layers** palette

STEP 10: Now that the shapes are drawn, you can define them as a pattern. Use the **Rectangular Marquee** tool to click and drag a selection marquee around the circles, beginning at the 0 point on both rulers and ending at the ⅞" point on both rulers. **8**

Step 11: To make the area around the circles transparent, turn off the *Background* layer's visibility. **9**

STEP 12: Because you need to select a non-shape layer before trying to define the pattern, select the *Background* layer. Then, from the **Edit** menu, choose **Define Pattern from Selection**. Name this pattern *digipattern2* and click **OK**.

That's it. Now the second pattern is finished and defined.

STEP 13: Save the entire master file as a PSD file (name it *digipatterns.psd*) and close it. You can use this file again later if you want to create more patterns.

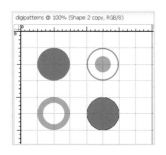

7 The shapes are in place.

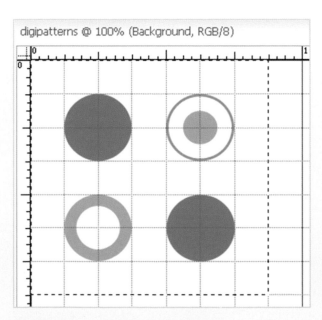

8 Select the area you want to use as a pattern.

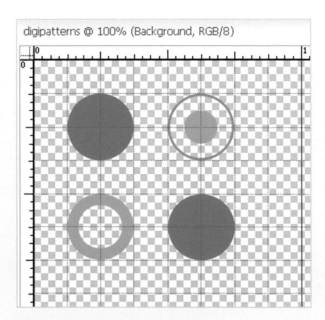

9 Turn off the background layer's visibility.

CREATING A DIGITAL BACKGROUND FROM YOUR PATTERN

Now it's time to create several 8 x 8 digital backgrounds using the first pattern you defined. To create the backgrounds, follow these steps.

STEP 1: Open a new blank file by opening the **File** menu and clicking **Blank File**. In the **Name** box, type *digibackgrounds*. Set the **Width** to 8" and the **Height** to 8". Set the **Resolution** to 300 pixels/inch, the **Color Mode** to RGB Color, and the **Background Contents** to White. Then click **OK**.

STEP 2: Turn off the grid by opening the View menu and clicking **Grid**.

STEP 3: To add a new layer, click the **Create a new layer** button at the top of the **Layers** palette. This layer will contain your first pattern. ❶

STEP 4: To fill the layer with the pattern you defined earlier, open the **Edit** menu and click **Fill Layer**. For **Use:** select **Pattern**. Then from the **Custom Pattern** drop-down list, select the first pattern you created, then click **OK**. ❷

STEP 5: To center the pattern on the document, select the **Move** tool, then use the **ARROW** keys on your keyboard to nudge the pattern across or up and down a few spaces until it's centered. Your first patterned background is complete! ❸

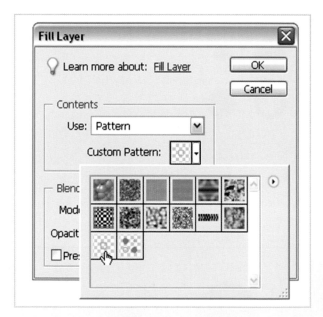

❷ Select the first pattern you created.

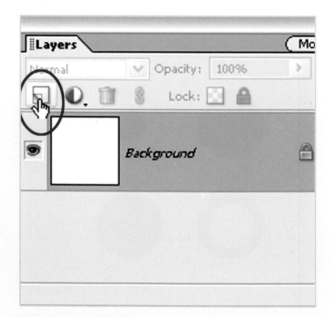

❶ The **Create a new layer** button.

STEP 6: Save this background as a **JPEG** file so that you can use it in later projects. From the **File** menu, point to **Save As**, and then name the new pattern file *pattern1bg1.jpg*. From the **Format** drop-down list, select **JPEG**. For **Format Options**, leave it set to the default **Baseline ("Standard")**. Then click **Save**. You may see a message saying the file must be saved as a copy. That's okay—it's just reminding you that instead of changing the original PSD file, you're creating a separate JPEG file, and that's exactly what you want to do, so click **OK**. In the **JPEG Options** window, set the quality to a minimum of **8 High** and click **OK**.

ⓣ TECH TIP

The quality of your printed output will be determined by a number of factors: paper, ink, and the resolution of the saved file. Save your JPEG files at the highest resolution you can afford. The higher the resolution, the larger the file, so make this decision based on how much hard drive space you have available. I strongly recommend a minimum of 8 High, but even higher if you can. Some digital scrapbookers have invested in external hard drives solely dedicated to storing their digital backgrounds and layouts.

ⓘ INFO TIP

You will generate several patterned background JPEG files from the master *digipatterns.psd* file, so you'll need to come up with a naming scheme for your files. Each JPEG file will be different, but they'll all be from the same family, so you may want your naming scheme to reflect that. You could use descriptive names, numbers, or whatever works for you. For the purposes of our exercises, we'll use really simple numeric names, but feel free to use your own names instead.

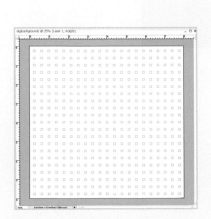

❸ The first completed patterned background.

CREATING MORE BACKGROUNDS FROM THE FIRST PATTERN

Remember how you created your original pattern with a transparent background? Now you can create a variety of new backgrounds from this pattern by simply changing the background colors. To do this, you'll add a new background layer and fill that background layer with a different color. Let's make a few more backgrounds now.

STEP 1: Add a new background layer by clicking the **Create a new layer** button in the **Layers** palette. Drag this layer down the stack until it's just above the *Background* layer.

STEP 2: From the **Window** menu, select **Color Swatches** to open up the color swatches you loaded earlier. Click **dark turquoise**. This loads the **Foreground Color** at the bottom of the toolbox with this color. ❶

STEP 3: Select the **Paint Bucket** tool. This tool fills an area or selection with the foreground color. Be sure the new layer is selected, then click once inside the document window. Voila! A new background.

STEP 4: Save this new background as a JPEG file (remember to keep the resolution at least 8 High.) Name it *pattern1bg2.jpg* (or any name you prefer). ❷ You may receive a message asking you if you'd like to save the file as part of a version set. If, when you use the Photo Browser, you'd like to see the edited version of the file displayed in a stack with the original file and other edited copies of it, say yes. If you want to see the edited copy by itself in another folder, for example, say no. It doesn't change the file—it just specifies whether or not it's displayed with the original.

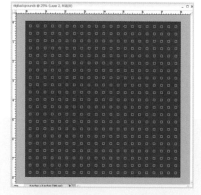

❷ The pattern now has a dark turquoise background.

❶ The foreground color is now dark turquoise.

❶ TECH TIP

At the bottom of the toolbox, you'll notice two color boxes. The top box contains the foreground color and the bottom box contains the background color. Photoshop Elements uses these two colors with a variety of tools. These boxes are always loaded with either the default colors (black and white) or colors you've selected by clicking on a color swatch or by using the **Eyedropper** tool to sample colors within your image. If you click the double-arrow next to the color boxes, the foreground and background colors will reverse. If you click inside either box, the **Color Picker** will open, allowing you to choose another color.

CREATING DIGITAL BACKGROUNDS FROM THE SECOND PATTERN

Now you'll use the second pattern you created to generate even more backgrounds. You're still using the same master .psd file. You'll just turn off the visibility of the first pattern layer and its turquoise background, since you don't need those layers right now, and you'll create new layers for the second pattern.

STEP 1: Turn off the visibility of the dark turquoise layer and the first pattern layer by clicking their eye icons in the **Layers** palette.

STEP 2: Click the **Create a new layer** button at the top of the **Layers** palette, and drag it to the top of the **Layers** palette. ❶

STEP 3: From the **Edit** menu, select **Fill Layer**. For **Use:** select **Pattern**. Then from the **Custom Pattern** drop-down list, select the second pattern you created, then click **OK**.

STEP 4: To center the pattern on the document, select the **Move** tool, then use the **ARROW** keys on your keyboard to nudge the pattern across or up and down a few spaces until it's centered. Your second patterned background is complete! ❷

STEP 5: Save this background as a JPEG file so that you can use it in later projects. From the **File** menu, point to **Save As**, and then name the new pattern file *pattern2bg1.jpg*. From the **Format** drop-down list, select **JPEG**. Then click Save. Remember to set the quality to a minimum of **8 High**.

❶ Create a new layer and drag it to the top of the **Layers** palette.

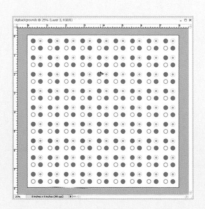

❷ The second patterned background is complete.

STEP 6: Why not create another background while you're at it? Turn on the visibility of the dark turquoise layer that's already in your **Layers** palette. Now save it as a JPEG file named *pattern2bg2.jpg*. That's it!

STEP 7: Start experimenting! Continue adding new layers, filling them with different colors to create new backgrounds for your patterns. Remember to move background layers of color below the pattern layers in the **Layers** palette. Turn off the visibility of layers you don't want showing, and turn on the visibility of layers you do want showing. Then save each combination of background color and pattern as a new JPEG file, and watch the variety of backgrounds in your collection increase painlessly!

I made six backgrounds from these two patterns. I added another solid layer and filled it with persimmon, then used that persimmon layer behind both patterns. You can see all six of my saved JPEG patterned backgrounds at the end of this lesson.

STEP 8: When you're finished creating digital backgrounds, be sure you save your master file as a PSD file before you close it. That will preserve all of the layers in case you want to use them again in new combinations later.

MANAGING YOUR PATTERNS
WITH THE PRESET MANAGER

As you develop more and more patterns, you're going to need a way to manage them. Photoshop Elements' **Preset Manager** is the perfect tool for this.

To use the **Preset Manager**, follow these steps.

STEP 1: From the **Edit** menu, select **Preset Manager**.

STEP 2: In the **Preset Type** box, select **Patterns**. You'll see the default patterns that came with Photoshop Elements, along with the two new patterns you added. ❶ Let's make a new set to contain only the patterns you created.

STEP 3: To select your patterns, press and hold **Shift** or **Ctrl** (**CMD** on a Mac) and click both patterns. Then click **Save Set**. Then name your set and click **Save**. I called mine *Renee Set 1*.

STEP 4: To reset the original set to the default patterns that came with Photoshop Elements, click the **More** button on the **Preset Manager** screen. Then select **Reset Patterns** and click **Done**.

STEP 5: Before your new set of patterns can appear in the **Preset Manager's** list, you must restart Photoshop Elements, so quit the program and restart it now.

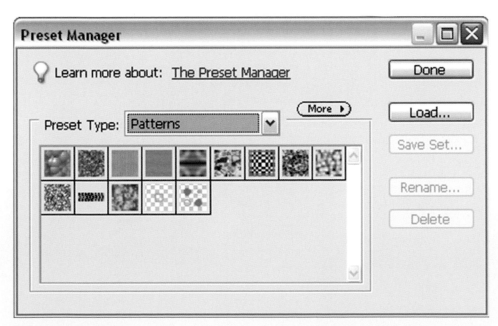

❶ The **Preset Manager**.

STEP 6: From the **Edit** menu, select **Preset Manager**. For the **Preset Type**, select **Patterns**. You'll notice that your patterns are no longer shown in the default list. That's because we moved them to their own list. Click the **More** button to display the list of additional pattern sets. Select your pattern set from the list. Your patterns are now ready to use. ❷

Congratulations! You've created your first digital patterned backgrounds from simple geometric designs you drew yourself. Now you have a lovely set of color-coordinated designs that look a lot more complex and difficult than they really are. Just imagine how impressed your friends will be!

Here are the six digital patterned backgrounds I created from our two patterns and three colored background layers (white, dark turquoise, and persimmon):

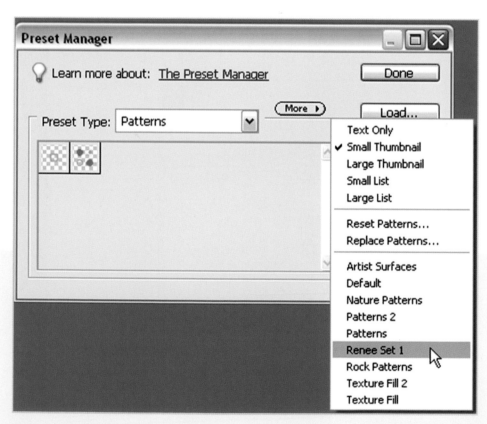

❷ Click the **More** button to select your pattern set from the list.

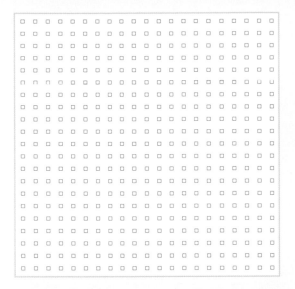
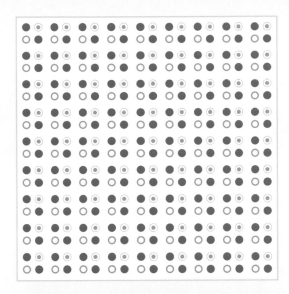
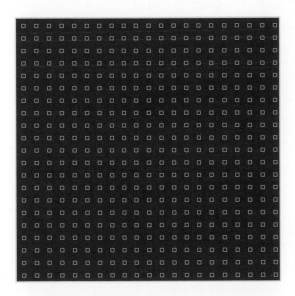
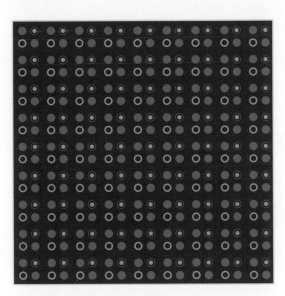
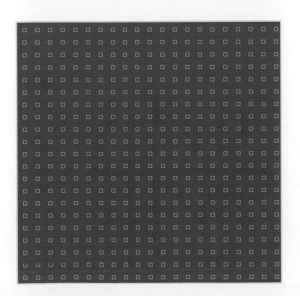
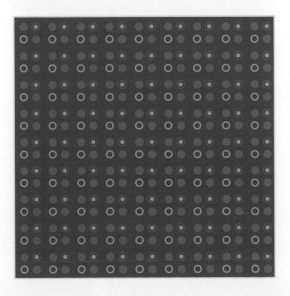

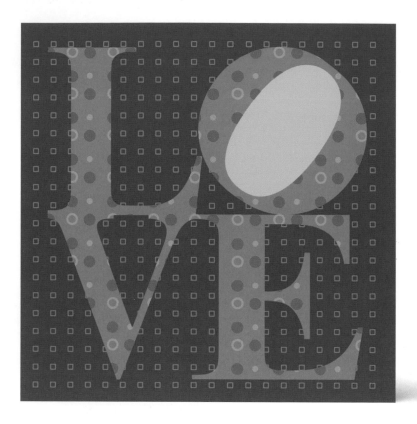

create backgrounds using type

Type isn't just for journaling anymore. Words, phrases, or even simple letters can form stunning backgrounds. Deceptively simple, type backgrounds can be subtle, striking, poignant, emotional, whimsical, elegant, bold, or just plain fun.

In this lesson, you'll make two completely different backgrounds using everyday fonts and a few simple techniques. First, you'll create a monochromatic background of subtle page-covering phrases with two larger title words for impact. Then you'll create a bold, bright background using only four letters in a familiar look.

USING TYPE AS AN ALL-OVER BACKGROUND

One theme I return to often is the idea of the many simple pleasures life has to offer. This theme is perfect for our first background page. Need a quick background to help tell a photo story? Transform your journaling into your background! Here's how.

STEP 1: Grab a sheet of paper and quickly list the simple pleasures in your life.

STEP 2: Open Photoshop Elements and go to the Editor workspace.

STEP 3: From the **File** menu, click **New** then **Blank File**. In the **Name** box, type *typebg1*. Set the **Width** to 8" and the **Height** to 8". Set the **Resolution** to 300 pixels/inch, the **Color Mode** to RGB Color, and the **Background Contents** to Transparent. Then click **OK**.

STEP 4: From the **View** menu, click **Fit On Screen** to enlarge the document to fit on the screen. If nothing happens, it's already sized to fit the screen.

STEP 5: If necessary, turn on the rulers by opening the **View** menu and clicking **Rulers**. You won't need the grid for this exercise, so you can leave it turned off.

STEP 6: You loaded the *Lolly* color swatches in the first lesson in this chapter. To open the **Color Swatches** palette, open the **Windows** menu and click **Color Swatches**.

STEP 7: Click the **Sage** swatch.

STEP 8: Select the **Paint Bucket** tool, then click once inside your document to fill the background layer *(Layer 1)* with color.

SIMPLE PLEASURES

THE SIMPLEST PLEASURES ARE THE BEST.
- GINGER PEACH TEA —— MORNING
- POPCORN AND A MOVIE
- SURF NET
- WATERMELON IN SUMMER
- AUTUMN
- CATS
- SUNDAY COMICS
- BRITISH SITCOMS
- FOOT RUBS
- BOOKSTORE
- THE SIMS
- LAVENDAR BATH

STEP 9: Select the **Horizontal Type** tool. **T** In the options bar, click **Color**, then choose **White**. This will make the text white when you type it.

STEP 10: Click and drag to draw a text box just inside your page boundaries. Make the box almost fill the page. ❶

STEP 11: Type the text you wrote earlier. For now, just use the default font and point size, and don't try to fill up the page. A few lines are all you need. ❷

ⓓ DESIGN TIP

For this background, a script font looks especially nice; I chose *French Script MT* for my example. I typed my text in all lower-case letters with no punctuation, but you can type it however you prefer.

STEP 12: Now you can change the font. To select all the text in the layer, either double-click the *Layer 2* thumbnail in the **Layers** palette, or use the **Horizontal Type** tool to click and drag from the beginning of the text to the end. ❸ Then choose a new font from the drop-down list in the options bar. Change the font's size to 30 points.

STEP 13: Adjust the spacing between the lines of text, called "leading," to give your text a little more breathing room. Choose a leading point size from the **Leading** drop-down list in the options bar. My example is set to 48 points. You may have to adjust the font size and the leading size if you use a different font. Just tweak it up and down 2 points at a time until you're satisfied with how the text looks. When you're finished, click the **Commit** checkmark on the right-hand side of the options bar to accept your changes.

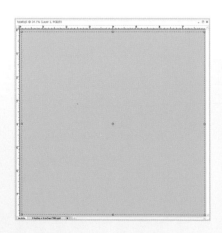

❶ Draw a text box just inside the page boundaries.

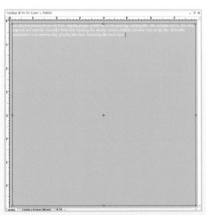

❷ Type the text you wrote earlier.

❸ Select the type by double-clicking *Layer 2* in the **Layers** palette.

STEP 14: Copy your text and paste it multiple times until the page is filled with the repeated text. ④ To do this, select all the text, then choose **Copy** from the **Edit** menu. Click once at the end of your existing text, type a space so the ending and beginning words don't run together, then paste the text by choosing **Paste** from the **Edit** menu. Keep pasting additional copies of the text until the page is filled. It's okay if the last copy of text runs off the page. When you're finished, click the **Commit** checkmark.

STEP 15: Expand the text box until your text bleeds off the sides of the page. To do this, first make sure you can see the boundaries of your text box. From the **View** menu, click **Zoom Out** until you can see the gray desktop surrounding your document. Now drag the lower right corner of the window until you can see about ⅛" of gray around the document.

Next, double-click the text layer's thumbnail in the **Layers** palette to select the text. Then drag the left and right handles until the text bleeds a little bit off the page. ⑤ When you're satisfied, click the **Commit** checkmark.

STEP 16: Select the **Move** tool, then use the **UP ARROW** and **DOWN ARROW** keys on your keyboard to adjust the text until it's centered vertically on the page. ⑥

④ Copy your text and paste it multiple times until the page is filled.

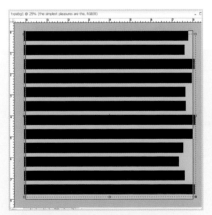

⑤ Drag the text box handles to make the text run slightly off the page.

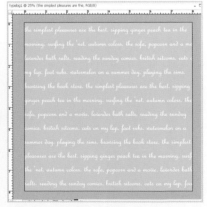

⑥ Select the **Move** tool and use the **ARROW** keys to center the text vertically.

STEP 17: To make the text less dominant on the page, lower its opacity. To do this, type 50% in the **Opacity** box at the top of the **Layers** palette. (You can also click the arrow beside the **Opacity** box and adjust the slider until the opacity is 50%.) **❼**

ⓘ INFO TIP
Lowering a layer's opacity means you're making the layer less opaque—in other words, more transparent. In this case, the text will look more faded because it will allow some of the background color to show through.

STEP 18: From the **View** menu, select **Fit on Screen** so that your page is easier to see.

ADDING MORE TEXT LAYERS

Now you'll overlay a couple of larger words for more design impact.

STEP 1: Turn off the visibility of your existing text layer so you don't accidentally select it.

STEP 2: Select the **Horizontal Type** tool, and click once inside your document. (It doesn't matter where, and it's okay if it runs off the page; you will move it around later.) Select the same font you used before, but change the font size to something very large. The example uses 264 points. Then change the font's color to **Lime**.

STEP 3: Type the word *simple* in lower-case letters. Then click the **Commit** checkmark. **❶**

STEP 4: Now you'll add a new word in a separate layer so that you can move this word independently from the first word. With the **Horizontal Type** tool,

❼ Reduce the text layer's opacity to 50%.

❶ Type the word *simple*.

click once again inside your document and type the word *pleasures* in lower-case letters. Notice that a new layer is created. Click the **Commit** checkmark. ❷

STEP 5: Select the **Move** tool, and make sure the **Auto Select Layer** and **Show Bounding Box** options are unchecked in the options bar.

STEP 6: Select the *simple* layer in the **Layers** palette, then click on the word *simple* and drag it to the upper left corner of the page, allowing a little of the word to bleed off the page.

STEP 7: Select the *pleasures* layer in the **Layers** palette, then click on the word *pleasures* and drag it to the bottom right corner of the page, again allowing a little to run off the page. ❸

STEP 8: To see your new background, turn on the visibility of the journaling text layer. ❹

STEP 9: From the **File** menu, click **Save As** to save this background as a JPEG file, with a minimum resolution of 8 High. You can name it *typebg1A.jpg*.

Your text background is finished!

❷ Type the word *pleasures*.

❸ Move the two words into position.

❹ Turn on the journaling text layer's visibility.

CREATING A VARIATION
OF YOUR TEXT BACKGROUND

Now you can combine this new background with one of the backgrounds you made in the first lesson, for a fun variation. Here's how.

STEP 1: Leave your text background file open. Then, from the **File** menu, click **Open** and select the patterned background with the four circles and dark turquoise background that you saved in the first lesson (*pattern2bg2.jpg*).

STEP 2: So that you can see both windows at the same time, click the **Automatically Tile Windows button** in the upper right corner of the screen (above the options bar, near the **Minimize** button. Then resize both windows so at least half of both are visible). **❶**

STEP 3: Click the *typebg1* document window to make it active. Then press **CTRL** (**CMD** on a Mac) and click the *simple* layer's thumbnail in the **Layers** palette. That will create a selection marquee around the word. **❷**

STEP 4: Using the **Rectangular Marquee** tool, click inside the selection marquee, then drag the selection marquee into the dark turquoise patterned background's window. **❸**

STEP 5: From the **Edit** menu, click **Copy**. This will copy the selected area of the pattern (in the shape of the word *simple*).

STEP 6: Click the type background's window to make it active again.

STEP 7: From the **Edit** menu, click **Paste**. This pastes a new layer—containing the word *simple* in the dark turquoise pattern—into the document.

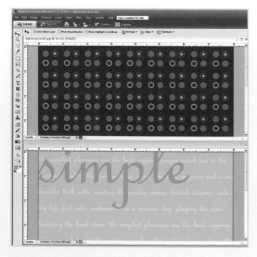

❶ Tile the windows so you can see both files.

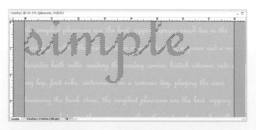

❷ The word *simple* is selected.

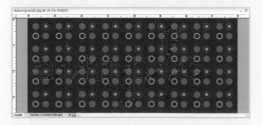

❸ Drag the selection marquee into the second window.

STEP 8: Use the **Move** tool to drag the new layer into the same position as the original *simple* layer.

STEP 9: Turn off the visibility of the original *simple* text layer. ❹

STEP 10: Repeat steps 3 - 9 to select, copy, and paste a patterned version of the word *pleasures* into your document. ❺

STEP 11: Save this version of your type background as a JPEG file named *typebg1B.jpg*.

STEP 12: Continue experimenting with type layers and text backgrounds. Save each combination you like as a JPEG file.

STEP 13: When you're finished, save your master type document as a PSD file so that you can continue to use all the layers later in other projects.

❺ The completed second type background.

❹ The patterned *simple* is now in the same position as the original *simple* text.

MAKING A "LOVE"LY BACKGROUND

Sources of inspiration for backgrounds using type are all around you. Magazines, catalogs, billboards... even postage stamps. This exercise was inspired by the Love postage stamp from the 1970s.

STEP 1: From the **File** menu, click **Blank File**. In the **Name** box, type *typebg2*. Set the **Width** to 8" and the **Height** to 8". Set the **Resolution** to 300 pixels/inch, the **Color Mode** to RGB Color, and the **Background Contents** to Transparent. Then click **OK**.

STEP 2: Turn on the rulers and the grid (use the **View** menu to toggle them on and off).

STEP 3: Select the **Horizontal Type** tool and choose a serif font, such as Times New Roman (which I used in the example).

STEP 4: In the boxes next to the font name in the options bar, set the font style to Bold, the point size to 408 points, and the color to **tangerine**.

STEP 5: Click once in the upper left section of the document window, then type the first letter, *L*, into your layout and click the **Commit** checkmark. Don't worry too much about where your letter is located—you'll move it around later. ❶

STEP 6: Click in the upper right section of the document and type the letter *O*, then click the **Commit** checkmark. This puts the letter *O* in a different layer than the letter *L*, so you can move them individually later.

STEP 7: In the lower left section, type the letter *V*, then click the **Commit**.

STEP 8: In the lower right section, type the letter *E*, then click the **Commit**.

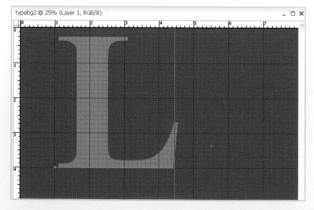

❶ Type the letter *L*.

ⓓ DESIGN TIP

Most typefaces are described as being "serif" or "sans serif" (without serifs). Serifs are the short lines that finish off the main strokes of letters. Some common serif typefaces are Times New Roman and Georgia. Common sans serif fonts are **Helvetica** and **Arial**. For this exercise, a serif font works best.

STEP 9: Select the **Move** tool, then one-by-one, click each letter's layer in the **Layers** palette and move the letter into position in the document. **②** Don't worry that they don't look like the arrangement on the postage stamp yet. Just move them roughly into position.

STEP 10: To make the O slanted, first select the O layer. Then from the **Image** menu, point to **Transform**, then click **Free Transform**. In the **Rotate** box in the options bar, type 45. **③** Then click **Commit**. **④**

ⓣ TECH TIP

There are two ways to rotate a layer's image. The easiest way is to type a specific degree of rotation in the **Rotate** box. (For this exercise, you're setting the O to a 45 degree angle, so type 45.) If you don't know exactly the degree by which you want to rotate the image, you can position the cursor near the lower left corner of the bounding box (the box that surrounds the selected image) until a curved

double-headed arrow appears. Then click and drag the cursor to rotate the image until you are satisfied.

STEP 11: Use the **Move** tool and the **ARROW** keys on your keyboard to move all the letters into position. Remember, to move each letter, you must first select its layer. This will be a trial-and-error process, as you move, nudge, and expand the letters until they fit against each other neatly.

First, move the slanted O until it butts against the L. When the two letters are touching, you may find they aren't the same height. Drag the corner or side handles on the bounding box around the letters to adjust the sizes until they match. **⑤** Refer to the grid to measure the height of each letter. Click **Commit** when you're satisfied.

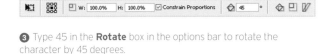

③ Type 45 in the **Rotate** box in the options bar to rotate the character by 45 degrees.

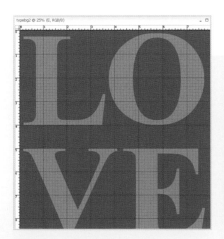

② Move the letters roughly into position.

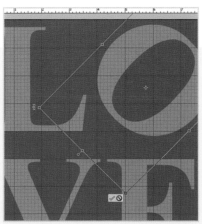

④ After rotating the letter O, click **Commit**.

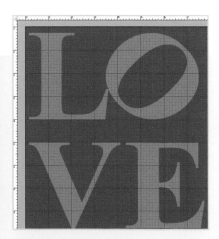

⑤ Move and adjust the letters L and O until they touch and are of equal height.

Use the same process to line up the V against the bottom of the L, and to position the E against both the slanted O and the V. Feel free to adjust their sizes until all four letters line up. You'll probably keep going back and forth between the letters to nudge and adjust until you're pleased with the result, so be patient. It will eventually look great! ❻

STEP 12: When all the letters are in position, you can copy the merged contents into a single layer. To do this, press and hold **CTRL** and **SHIFT** (**CMD** and **SHIFT** on a Mac) and click each letter's thumbnail in the **Layers** palette. When you've selected the thumbnails of all four layers, open the **Edit** menu and click **Copy Merged**. Then choose **Paste** from the **Edit** menu. Then new merged layer will appear in the **Layers** palette.

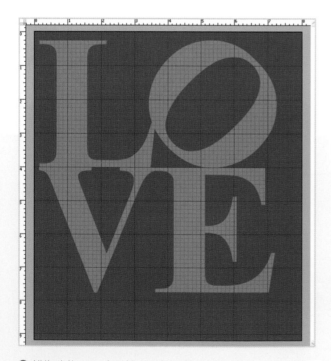

❻ All the letters are touching and sized to match.

ⓣ TECH TIP

Copying and merging the contents of several layers into one makes it easier to work with all the letters at once, and keeps you from accidentally moving one layer and having to start all over. Your original letter layers will still be there, should you make a mistake and need to try again, or in case you want to modify them individually later. You'll turn off their visibility so they don't confuse you, but they'll still be there in the master PSD file.

STEP 13: Drag the new layer to the top of the **Layers** palette, and rename it *merged type*.

STEP 14: Turn off the visibility of the four individual type layers.

STEP 15: Select the new *merged type* layer.

STEP 16: If your letters aren't centered exactly in your document, use the **Move** tool and the **ARROW** keys to nudge the layer into place. ❼

ⓘ INFO TIP

Naming your layers as you create them helps you identify the layers you're looking for as your **Layers** palette grows. To change a layer's name, double-click the layer's default name in the **Layers** palette, then type the new name.

STEP 17: From the **Image** menu, point to **Transform**, then click **Free Transform**. In the options bar, make sure the **Constrain Proportions** box is checked. Then change either the width or height to 90%. The other dimension will change automatically (the result of that **Constrain Proportions** box!), and the merged layer will shrink a little. Click **Commit**. ❽

STEP 18: Click the **Create a new layer** button in the **Layers** palette, and name the layer *pattern love*.

STEP 19: In the **Layers** palette, drag the *pattern love* layer until it is positioned just above the *merged type* layer.

STEP 20: Press **CTRL** (**CMD** on a Mac) and click the *merged type* thumbnail. This puts a selection marquee around the letters.

STEP 21: From the **Edit** menu, click **Fill Selection**.

STEP 22: For **Use**, select **Pattern**, then choose your second pattern (the four circles) from the drop-down list. Click **OK**.

STEP 23: Press **ESC** to remove the selection marquee (or choose **Deselect** from the **Select** menu). ❾

Now your letters have a pattern fill!

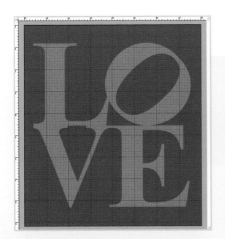

❼ Center the letters in the document.

❽ Shrink the merged layer to 90% of its original size

❾ Fill the selection with the pattern you made in Lesson 1.

FILLING THE CENTER OF THE LETTER O

Now that the main design of your "Love" background is complete, you can add a few more decorative elements to finish the look.

STEP 1: First, let's fill the center of the letter O with a solid color. To begin, create a new layer, name it *fill*, and drag it into position just below the *merged type* layer. ❶

STEP 2: Select the merged type layer. Then select the **Magic Wand** tool and click inside the center of the slanted O in the document. Now the inside of the O is selected. ❷

STEP 3: Select the *fill* layer.

STEP 4: To make sure none of the background peeks through, expand the selection (the inside of the O). To do this, open the **Select** menu, then point to **Modify**, then click **Expand**. Set **Expand By** to 4 pixels. Click **OK**.

STEP 5: Select **Sage** from the **Color Swatches** palette.

STEP 6: Select the **Paint Bucket** tool and click inside the selection (the center of the O). The area behind the center of the slanted O is now filled with color. ❸

STEP 7: Press **ESC** to remove the selection marquee.

❶ Create a new layer named *fill* just below the *merged type* layer.

❷ Use the **Magic Wand tool** to select the inside of the letter O.

❸ The center of the letter O is filled with sage.

❶ TECH TIP

The Magic Wand tool selects pixels within a color range. It's great for selecting solid color areas.

ADDING A PATTERNED BACKGROUND

Now you can add a pattern to the background.

STEP 1: Create a new layer, name it *pattern background* and drag it to the bottom of the **Layers** palette, just above the persimmon background layer.

STEP 2: Fill this layer with the first pattern you created in Lesson 1. To do this, open the **Edit** menu and click **Fill Layer**. For **Use**, select **Pattern**, then choose the first pattern you made earlier. ❶

STEP 3: Remember how this pattern you created earlier has a transparent background? You now need to lock those transparent pixels so that they remain transparent while you're changing other aspects of the layer. Click the **Lock Transparent Pixels** button at the top of the **Layers** palette. A small lock icon will appear in the layer. ❷

ⓘ TECH TIP

Locking a layer's transparent pixels ensures that its transparent areas don't get filled with color when you change another element in that layer. At the top of the **Layers** palette, you'll see the word "**Lock**" and two buttons: a padlock (which says "**Lock all**" when you position the cursor over it) and a small square (which says "**Lock transparent pixels**" when you position the cursor over it). Click the square button (the **Lock transparent pixels** button) to lock just the transparent pixels so they stay transparent. If you click the **Padlock** icon, the entire layer will be locked and you won't be able to change anything at all in the layer.

STEP 4: In the **Color Swatches** palette, click **tangerine**.

STEP 5: From the **Edit** menu, click **Fill** Layer. For **Use**, select **Foreground Color.** Then click **OK**. This changes the color of the pattern to tangerine.

STEP 6: In the **Layers** palette, reduce the pattern background layer's **Opacity** to 60%. ❸

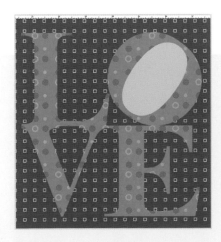

❶ Fill the layer with the pattern you created in Lesson 1.

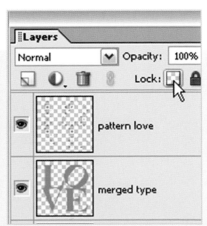

❷ Click the **Lock Transparent Pixels** button.

❸ Reduce the pattern background layer's opacity to 60%.

ADDING A FRAME

Now you'll add a ¼" frame around the page, in the same persimmon color as the background itself. This will make a subtle border instead of letting the circle pattern bleed off the edge of the page. It will help give your page a polished, bounded look.

STEP 1: Create a new layer, name it *frame*, and drag it into position just above the *pattern background* layer you just filled.

STEP 2: Use the **Rectangular Marquee** tool to draw a selection marquee beginning at the ¼" points on both rulers and ending at the 7 ¾" points on both rulers. **❶**

STEP 3: From the **Select** menu, click **Inverse**. This reverses the selected area so that instead of the inner rectangle being selected, now the outer border of the page is selected.

STEP 4: Click the **Paint Bucket** tool, choose the **persimmon** color, and click the selected area to fill it with persimmon.

STEP 5: Select the *pattern background* layer, then use the **Move** tool and the **ARROW** keys to center it within this new frame. **❷**

STEP 6: Turn off the grid, and admire your new background! Your second type background is now finished.

STEP 7: Save this background as a JPEG file, named *typebg2A.jpg*.

STEP 8: Save the entire master file as a PSD file *(typebg2.psd)*, and then close the file. You're finished with this one for now.

Congratulations! You've completed another set of beautiful backgrounds.

Next you'll be trying some creative layering techniques to create even more designs.

❶ Draw a selection marquee ¼" from each edge of the document.

❷ Center the *pattern background* layer within the frame.

LESSON 3

creative layering techniques

This lovely background image may look complex,
but this book's CD contains all the building blocks
you need to create this layered composition.
Using those building blocks, along with Photoshop
Elements' blending modes, you'll be surprised at
just how easy it is to create this background.

USING EXISTING FILES TO CREATE LAYERS

Instead of starting from a new, blank file, you'll open and use one of the gradient backgrounds provided on the CD. This is a fast and easy starting point for almost any layered background you want to create.

STEP 1: Open Photoshop Elements and go to the Editor workspace.

STEP 2: From the **File** menu, click **Open** and open the *gradientorg8.jpg* file from the backgrounds folder on this book's CD. ❶

STEP 3: Because you're going to start adding layers to this file, save it as a PSD file, and name it *layeredbg1.psd*.

STEP 4: From the **View** menu, turn on the rulers and the grid, and fit the document to the screen **(Fit on Screen)**.

STEP 5: You loaded the Lolly color swatches in the first lesson in this chapter. To open this **Color Swatches** palette, open the **Windows** menu and click **Color Swatches**.

STEP 6: The first thing you'll do is add a "distressed" semi-transparent layer to roughen up the background and give it that "grunge" look. From the **File** menu, click **Place**. Then navigate to the *distressed.png* file in the *other* folder on the CD. Click **Place.** The artwork from the *distressed.png* file appears inside a bounding box at the center of your document. ❷

You could have opened the *distressed.png* file, copied it, and pasted it into your document like you did in previous lessons. With Photoshop Elements, there's often more than one way to do something. In this particular case, using the **Place** command to place the file into the document is easier because the **Place** command automatically resizes the distressed file from its original 12 x 12 size to fit

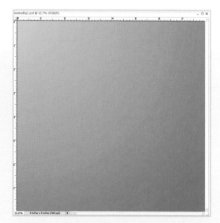

❶ Open the *gradientorg8.jpg* file on the CD.

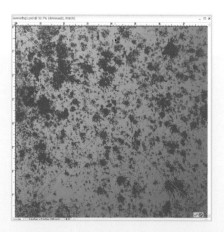

❷ **Place** the *distressed.png* file into your document.

inside your 8 x 8 image, while maintaining the original file's aspect ratio (the image's height-to-width relationship).

STEP 7: At this point, you could reposition or resize the new artwork. However, for this lesson, just press **ENTER** or click the **Commit** checkmark to accept the image as it is.

STEP 8: Now you will load two colors into the **Foreground** and **Background** color boxes at the bottom of the toolbox. The top box contains the foreground color and the bottom box contains the background color. If you click the **double-arrow** next to the color boxes, the foreground and background colors will reverse. To load a color into one of the boxes, click the color in the **Color Swatches** palette. That loads that color into the **Foreground** box. Then click the **double-arrow** to move that color to the **Background** box. Finally, click another color to load *it* into the **Foreground** box.

For this exercise, we want persimmon to be the background color and sage to be the foreground color. So first, click **persimmon** in the **Color Swatches** palette. Next, click the **double-arrow** by the color boxes to move persimmon to the **Background** color box. Then click **sage**. Notice that the foreground color in the toolbox is now sage.

STEP 9: Make sure the *distressed* layer is still selected, then click the **Lock transparent pixels** button.

STEP 10: Fill the *distressed* layer with the foreground color (sage). To do this, open the **Edit** menu, click **Fill Layer**, and for **Use** select **Foreground Color**. ❸

STEP 11: Reduce the *distressed* layer's opacity to 25%. ❹

❸ Fill the distressed layer with sage.

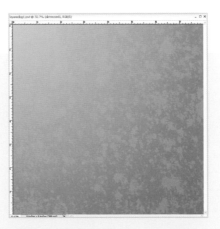

❸ Reduce the *distressed* layer's opacity to 25%.

STEP 12: With just two layers, you already have a nicely textured background to work with, so save this as a JPEG file so you can use it later if you'd like.

But don't close the master file. We're not finished yet!

ADDING ANOTHER DECORATIVE LAYER

Now you'll add another layer with a decorative element.

STEP 1: From the **File** menu, click **Place**, then select the *ovrly2.png* file from the **elements** folder on the CD. **1**

STEP 2: Now you'll copy this element and create another one in a new layer. To do this, first use the **Magic Wand** tool and click inside the white area of the decorative design. (It's okay if a few smaller pieces of white in the design are not selected.)

STEP 3: Click the **Create a new layer** button in the **Layers** palette. From the **Edit** menu, click **Fill Selection**. For **Use**, select **Background Color**. This will automatically create a new persimmon version of the design in the new layer. Press **ESC** to remove the selection marquee. **2**

STEP 4: Next you'll flip this new element on the page. From the **Image** menu, point to **Rotate**, then click **Flip Layer Vertical**. Because you only want to flip this one layer, be sure you select **Flip Layer Vertical**, which is near the bottom of the menu, and not **Flip Vertical**. **Flip Vertical** will flip all the layers in the file.

STEP 5: Use the **Move** tool to move the persimmon element to the upper right corner of your page. **3**

1 Place the *ovrly2.png* file into your document.

2 Make a new copy of the decorative element and fill it with persimmon.

3 Flip and reposition the persimmon design layer.

USING BLENDING MODES

Now you'll enhance the elements on your page
by using blending modes.

STEP 1: Make sure the persimmon design layer
is still selected.

STEP 2: At the top of the **Layers** palette, click
the drop-down list of blending modes. A layer's
blending mode determines how its pixels blend
with the underlying pixels in the image. You can
create a variety of interesting effects with blending
modes. Experiment with them! Try out several of
the blending modes before moving on to the next
step. Some examples are shown on this page. For
more information on blending modes, see the
Adobe Photoshop Elements Help. ❶ ❷ ❸

❶ The **Screen** blending mode.

❷ The **Multiply** blending mode..

❸ The **Color Dodge** blending mode.

STEP 2: When you're finished experimenting, select the **Hard Light** blending mode. The effect of the Hard Light blending mode is similar to shining a harsh spotlight on the layer, and it's the blending mode you'll use for this exercise. ④

STEP 4: The final step is to add a distressed frame to your background. From the **File** menu, click **Place**, then select the *frame.png* file from the other folder on the CD. Click **Commit**. ⑤

STEP 5: Make sure the new layer is selected, and click the **Lock transparent pixels** button.

STEP 6: To fill the layer with persimmon, open the **Edit** menu and click **Fill Layer**. For **Use**, select **Background Color** (which should still be persimmon).

STEP 7: From the **Blending mode** drop-down list, click **Soft Light**. This will soften the frame. ⑥

STEP 8: Your background is now complete, so save it as a JPEG file.

STEP 9: To preserve all the layers in case you want to use them again in another project, save the master file as a PSD file.

That's it! You've just created a gorgeous layered background from some simple building blocks on this book's CD. Later in this book, you'll learn how to use the building blocks with more advanced layering techniques.

But for now, let's move on to creating digital embellishments.

④ The **Hard Light** blending mode.

⑤ **Place** the *frame.png* file into the document.

⑥ Apply the **Soft Light** blending mode to the frame layer.

creating digital embellishments

In the scrapbooking world, embellishments such as brads, tags, and bookplates are tremendously popular, because they give a page that extra bit of visual and textural interest. Just because you're creating digital scrapbooks instead of paper pages doesn't mean you have to go without those fun extra touches. In fact, with Adobe Photoshop Elements, you have unlimited choices in creating your own digital elements to match your own sense of style, color, and design.

In this chapter, you'll learn just how easy it is to create your own digital embellishments, called "elements" in the digital scrapbooking world. In the first lesson, you'll use templates I've provided to create three of the most popular embellishments: brads, tags, and bookplates. In the second lesson, you'll learn how to create your own "from scratch." In the third lesson, you'll tackle making digital chipboard, which is a lot easier than you may think. Let's get started!

create embellishments from templates

An easy way to learn about creating and modifying digital elements is to begin with the templates on this book's CD.

Let's start with brads. In this exercise, you'll use the brad template I've provided, then you'll change its color, background and size to make a variety of brads that you can use in your future scrapbook projects.

Just as with the background exercises in Chapter 1, at the end of this exercise, you'll have created a single master PSD file with lots of layers in it so that you can continue to modify those layers in the future if you want to. In addition, after you have created a variety of brads from those layers, you will save a PNG version of the file. The PNG version will be the version from which you can copy completed brads to paste into your scrapbook projects.

CREATING BRADS FROM A TEMPLATE

My simple brad template will let you create brads in a variety of colors, textures, and patterns.

STEP 1: Open Photoshop Elements and go to the Editor workspace.

STEP 2: Open the file *dds2brad.psd* from the *templates* folder on the CD that came with this book. ❶

STEP 3: Before you modify the brad, save this file with a different filename (PSD format) to your hard disk so that you can always return to the original if you need to.

STEP 4: Open the **Color Swatches** palette (from the **Window** menu, click **Color Swatches**). The Lolly color swatches should still be loaded from the exercises you completed earlier. If not, load them, as explained in the first exercise in Chapter 1.

STEP 5: Click the **lime** swatch. This changes the foreground color box in the toolbox to lime.

STEP 6: Make sure the *brad* layer is selected in the **Layers** palette. Notice that the **Lock transparent pixels** icon appears beside the layer's icon. ❷ This means the transparent portions of the layer will stay transparent when you apply a new color to the layer.

STEP 7: From the **Edit** menu, click **Fill Layer**. For **Use**, select **Foreground color**. The brad is now lime green! ❸

There you have it! That's how easy it is to make digital brads in the colors of your choice. But you're not limited to using solid colors for your brads. You can also use decorative backgrounds to add patterns to your brads.

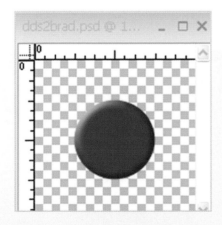

❶ Open the brad template file, *dds2brad.psd*.

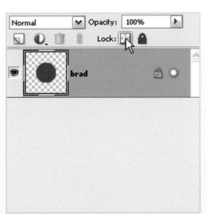

❷ The layer's transparent pixels are locked.

❸ The brad color changes to lime.

ADDING A DECORATIVE BACKGROUND TO A BRAD

To add a pattern to your brad, you can use one of the decorative *backgrounds* from the CD. First you'll open the decorative background, then you'll resize it before applying it to the background.

STEP 1: Open the *swooshyswirly8.jpg* file from the backgrounds folder on the CD. ❶

STEP 2: From the **Image** menu, point to **Resize**, then click **Image Size**. In the dialog box that appears, make sure the **Resample Image** box is checked. Then set both the width and height to ½". (That's the same size as the brad template document.) Then click **OK**.

STEP 3: From the **Select** menu, click **All** to select the entire background.

STEP 4: From the **Edit** menu, click **Copy**.

STEP 5: Close the background file (don't save any changes). You won't need it anymore for this exercise.

STEP 6: Click the brad document to make it active, then from the **Edit** menu, click **Paste**. ❷ The decorative layer completely covers the brad, so next we'll trim away the excess.

STEP 7: Make sure the decorative layer you just copied is selected. Then press **CTRL** (**CMD** on a Mac) and click inside the *brad* layer's thumbnail in the **Layers** palette. (Make sure you click in the *brad* layer's thumbnail, not the decorative layer.) A circular shape is selected in the decorative layer.

STEP 8: From the **Select** menu, click **Inverse**. Now the excess around the circle is selected.

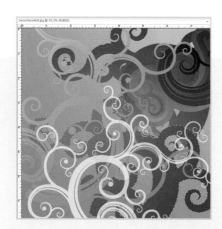

❶ Open the background file, *swooshyswirly8.jpg*.

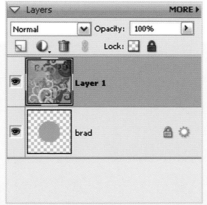

❷ Paste the decorative layer onto the brad document.

❸ The excess is cut away.

STEP 9: From the **Edit** menu, click **Cut**. The excess disappears, and you have the circular shape you need. **3**

STEP 10: Select the *brad* layer in the **Layers** palette. Then, from the **Layer** menu, point to **Layer Style**, then click **Copy Layer Style**. **4**

STEP 11: Select the decorative layer (*Layer 1*) in the **Layers** palette.

STEP 12: From the **Layer** menu, point to **Layer Style**, then click **Paste Layer Style**. **5**

Now your brad has a pattern and looks three-dimensional. Don't close the file yet. Now that you know how to recolor the brad template, why not create an entire collection of brads in different colors and sizes in a single document? That way, they're easy to find when you want to use them later.

d **DESIGN TIP**

When I created the brad template, I applied a Layer Style to the brad to make it look three-dimensional. When you use this template to create your own brads, you copy that Layer Style onto your circles to give them the same look. You'll learn more about Layer Styles and how to use them to create your own embellishments later in this chapter.

4 From the **Layer** menu, choose **Copy Layer Style**.

5 Paste the **Layer Style** onto the decorative layer.

CREATING MORE BRADS

You've already created two brads. Using the same techniques, now you'll create two more solid color brad layers. The easiest way to create more solid color brads is to duplicate the brad layer, then fill the duplicate with a new color. The following steps show how.

STEP 1: Turn off the visibility of the decorative brad layer (*Layer 1*) by clicking that layer's eye icon.

STEP 2: Select the **persimmon** swatch from the **Color Swatches** palette.

STEP 3: Select the original *brad* layer in the **Layers** palette.

STEP 4: Click the **MORE** arrow at the top of the **Layers** palette, then click **Duplicate Layer** from the drop-down list. ❶

STEP 5: Name the new layer *brad persimmon* and click **OK**.

STEP 6: From the **Edit** menu, click **Fill** Layer. For **Use**, select **Foreground Color** and click **OK**. Now you have a persimmon brad!

STEP 7: Now you'll make a banana-colored brad. First, turn off the visibility of your new persimmon brad.

STEP 8: Repeat steps 2 through 6, using **banana**.

Now you have four brad layers in your file—three solid colors and one with the decorative pattern.

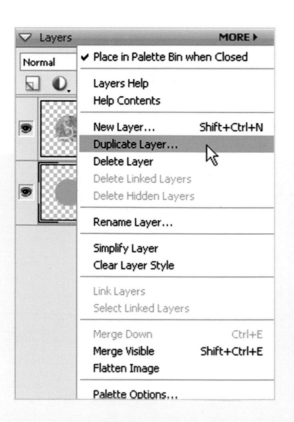

❶ From the **MORE** drop-down list, select **Duplicate Layer**.

CREATING A BRADS COLLECTION

Now that you've created four brads in your master PSD file, you can arrange them in a new document so they'll be easier to use in your scrapbooking projects. You will also make more of the same brads in smaller sizes. That way, you have a choice of ⅛" or ¼" brads when you're ready to use them. This is exactly what I did to create the sets in the elements folder on the CD.

STEP 1: Turn off the visibility of all layers except the original brad layer. It doesn't matter which layer is selected in the **Layers** palette.

STEP 2: From the **Select** menu, click **All**.

STEP 3: From the **Edit** menu, click **Copy Merged**.

STEP 4: Create a new blank file (from the **File** menu, point to **New**, then click **Blank File**). Name the file *bradset*, set the **Width** to 1 ¼", the **Height** to ¾", the **Resolution** to 300 pixels, and the **Background** to transparent. ❶

STEP 5: Use the **View** menu to turn on the rulers and the grid. To set the grid subdivision size, open the **Edit** menu, point to **Preferences**, click **Grid**, and set the **Subdivisions** to 4.

STEP 6: From the **Edit** menu, click **Paste**. The lime brad appears in your new document. ❷

STEP 7: Because this first brad is ¼", let's make a smaller ⅛" version so you'll have a choice of sizes and won't have to resize it every time you need a smaller one. First, make sure the lime brad's layer (*Layer 1*) is selected.

STEP 8: In the **Layers** palette, click the **MORE** arrow and select **Duplicate Layer**.

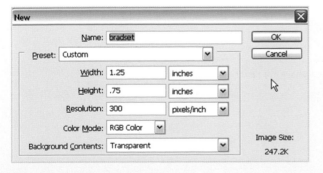

❶ Create a new blank file named *bradset*.

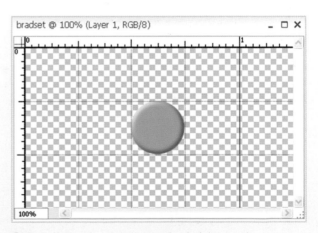

❷ Paste the lime brad into the new *bradset* document.

STEP 9: Give the new layer a name and click **OK**. ❸

STEP 10: Select the duplicate layer in the **Layers** palette.

STEP 11: From the **Image** menu, point to **Transform**, then click **Free Transform**.

STEP 12: In the options bar, make sure the **Constrain Proportions** button is checked. Then right-click inside the width box (labeled **W**) and select inches from the drop-down list of units.

STEP 13: Change the width to 0.125 inches. (Don't worry about the height; it will automatically change to match the width.) ❹

STEP 14: Click the **Commit** checkmark. Now you have two brads in your document: one is ¼" and the other is ⅛". ❺

STEP 15: Use the **Move** tool to move the brads into the upper left corner of the document, so there will be more room for additional brads. (To move a brad, select that brad's layer in the **Layers** palette, then use the **Move** tool or the **ARROW** keys.) ❻

STEP 16: Now you'll repeat all these steps to copy more brads into the document. First, return to the original document and turn off the visibility of all the layers except for the persimmon brad layer.

STEP 17: From the **Select** menu, click **All**.

STEP 18: From the **Edit** menu, click **Copy Merged**, then paste the copied brad into the new document (the same document with the lime brads in it).

STEP 19: Select the persimmon brad layer and duplicate it. (Remember, to duplicate a layer, click the **MORE** arrow in the **Layers** palette.)

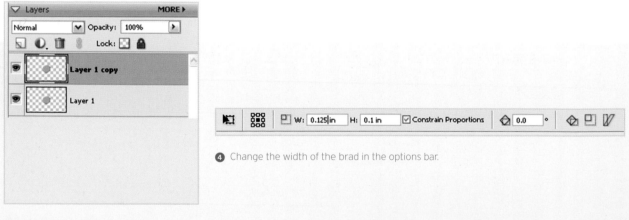

❸ Duplicate the brad layer.

❹ Change the width of the brad in the options bar.

STEP 20: From the **Image** menu, use **Free Transform** to shrink the duplicated brad and then click the **Commit** checkmark.

STEP 21: Use the **Move** tool to move the brads to a convenient place in the document.

STEP 22: Repeat steps 16 through 21 for the banana and decorative brads. When you're finished, you should have eight brads—four ¼" and four ⅛" brads. ❼

STEP 23: From the **File** menu, click **Save As**, then specify the PNG file format. Saving this file as a PNG file will preserve the transparency around the brads. This PNG file will be the file you open to use these brads in future scrapbook projects. You'll use one of the **Marquee** tools to select a brad, then **Copy** and **Paste** just that single brad into your page layout.

ⓣ **TECH TIP**

PNG (Portable Network Graphics) files save transparent backgrounds. To preserve the transparency around the brads for future use in layouts, be sure you save your brads file in the PNG file format.

Congratulations! You've created your first digital brads. Feel free to experiment with more sizes and colors. Create multiple sets of brads in coordinated colors and patterns, and save each set as a PNG file to use later.

When you're finished, save and close both your PNG file and your master PSD file. (Remember, you'll still have a brad template on the CD with the original brad on it, should you need it.)

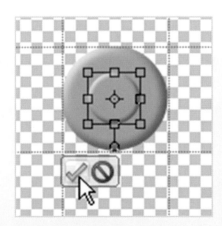

❺ The duplicated brad is ⅛".

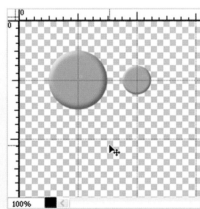

❻ Use the **Move** tool to move the brads into the upper left corner of the document.

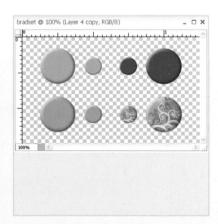

❼ The finished document should contain all eight brads.

CREATING DIGITAL BOOKPLATES FROM A TEMPLATE

Metal bookplates are very popular, and for good reason. They make a lovely frame for a title, journaling, or even a special image. Now you can make a digital version of a bookplate using the template on this book's CD.

The bookplate template is a little more complex than the brad template. Because the bookplate template is made of multiple layers, you'll need to select and re-color each layer one at a time. The steps and techniques, however, are the same as the one you used with the brads.

STEP 1: Open the file *dds2bkplate.psd* from the templates folder on the CD.

STEP 2: Before you modify the bookplate, save this file with a different filename (PSD format) to your hard disk so that you can always return to the original if you need to.

STEP 3: Open the **Color Swatches** palette (from the **Window** menu, click **Color Swatches**).

STEP 4: Click the **persimmon** swatch. This changes the foreground color box in the toolbox.

STEP 5: Select the *top bevel* layer in the **Layers** palette. Notice that the layer's transparent pixels are locked.

STEP 7: From the **Edit** menu, click **Fill Layer** and fill the layer with the **Foreground color**. ❶

STEP 8: Continue selecting and filling each layer with persimmon until the entire bookplate is persimmon. ❷

❶ TECH TIP

Instead of using the Edit menu each time you want to fill a layer with color, you can use a keyboard shortcut. Press **ALT** and **DEL** to make quick work of filling a selected layer.

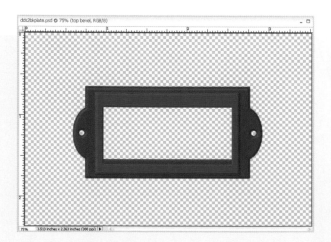

❶ The *top bevel* layer is now persimmon.

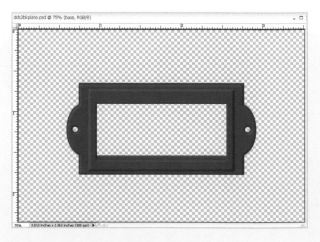

❷ Paste the decorative layer onto the brad document.

CREATING MORE BOOKPLATES

You've already created one bookplate in persimmon. Using the same techniques, now you'll create two more solid color bookplates. The easiest way to create more solid color bookplates is to duplicate all the bookplate layers, then fill each duplicate with the new color. The following steps show how.

STEP 1: Select the **lemon** swatch from the **Color Swatches** palette.

STEP 2: Select all four of the original layers at once by pressing **CTRL** (**CMD** on a **Mac**) while you click each layer in the **Layers** palette. ❶

STEP 3: Click the **MORE** arrow at the top of the **Layers** palette, then click **Duplicate Layers**.

STEP 4: Select the *top bevel copy* layer and fill it with lemon. Then repeat for each of the other three layer copies.

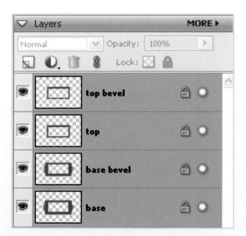

❶ Select the four original bookplate layers.

STEP 5: Select **sage** from the **Color Swatches** palette, and repeat steps 2 through 4 to make a sage bookplate.

Now you have three solid-color bookplates in your file, each of which uses four layers. Next, you can make a bookplate using a decorative background. ❷

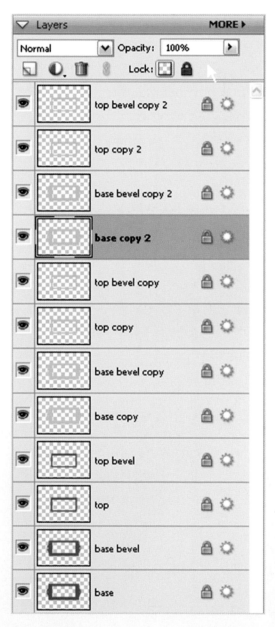

❷ The **Layers** palette has two more solid-color bookplates.

ADDING A DECORATIVE
BACKGROUND TO A BOOKPLATE

To add a pattern to your bookplate, you can use one of the decorative backgrounds from the CD. First you'll open the decorative background, then you'll resize it before applying it to the background.

STEP 1: Open the *swooshygreen8.jpg* file from the *backgrounds* folder on the CD.

STEP 2: From the **Image** menu, point to **Resize**, then click **Image Size**. In the dialog box that appears, make sure the **Resample Image** box is checked. Then set both the width and height to 3 ½" (so it's closer to the size of the bookplate template document). Then click **OK**.

STEP 3: From the **Select** menu, click **All** to select the entire background.

STEP 4: From the **Edit** menu, click **Copy**.

STEP 5: Close the background file (don't save any changes). You won't need it anymore for this exercise.

STEP 6: Click the bookplate document to make it active, and select the highest layer in the **Layers** palette (so that the new layer you're about to paste in goes at the top of the stack). Then from the **Edit** menu, click **Paste**. The decorative layer completely covers the bookplate.

STEP 7: Make sure the decorative layer you just pasted in is selected. Then duplicate that decorative layer three more times, so that there are four decorative layers.

STEP 8: Select the top decorative layer you just created.

STEP 9: Press **CTRL** (**CMD** on a **Mac**) and click inside the original *top bevel* layer's thumbnail in the **Layers** palette. (Make sure you click in the *top bevel* layer's thumbnail, not the decorative layer.) The top bookplate shape is selected in the decorative layer.

STEP 10: From the **Select** menu, click **Inverse**. Now the excess around the bookplate is selected.

STEP 11: From the **Edit** menu, click **Cut**. The excess disappears, and you have the bookplate shape you need. (It will still look solid, however, because the three lower decorative layers are still visible. Look at the thumbnail for your layer in the **Layers** palette—you'll see that the bookplate shape is indeed all that remains in that layer.)

STEP 12: Because you resized the decorative background file to 3 ½ x 3 ½, which is larger than the template file, some of that pasted background is outside the boundaries of the bookplate document. It's good practice to remove excess from the outside boundaries of a document. While it may not be visible, it unnecessarily adds to your file size. To clean that up, select **All** from the **Select** menu. Then from the **Image** menu, click **Crop**.

Now everything outside the boundaries of the document window has been deleted. Press **ESC** to remove the selection marquee.

STEP 13: Repeat steps 7 through 12 for the other three decorative layers, choosing a different original bookplate layer each time to select and trim that shape.

STEP 14: Now you must copy the Layer Style from each of the original bookplate layers to their corresponding decorative bookplate layers. Earlier, you learned how to use the **Layer** menu to copy and paste Layer Styles from an original layer to the decorative layer. A faster method is to press **ALT** while dragging the **Styles** icon from the original layer to the destination layer. The Styles icon is located next to the layer's name in the **Layers** palette. It looks like a splat in Photoshop Elements 5.0 or an italicized "f" in Photoshop Elements 4.0. Remember to press **ALT** while dragging the **Styles** icon from each of the four original layers to each of the four new decorative layers.

There! Now you have four different bookplates (each made of four separate layers). Next, you will create a PNG document and paste your bookplates into it.

CREATING A NEW BOOKPLATES COLLECTION

Just as you did with your brads, now you can arrange your bookplates in a new document so they'll be easier to use in your scrapbooking projects. You will also make more of the same bookplates in smaller sizes.

STEP 1: Turn off the visibility of all layers except the original four persimmon bookplate layers. It doesn't matter which layer is selected in the **Layers** palette.

STEP 2: From the **Select** menu, click **All**.

STEP 3: From the **Edit** menu, click **Copy Merged**.

STEP 4: Create a new blank file (from the **File** menu, point to **New**, then click **Blank File**). Name the file *bookplateset*, set the **Width** to 6", the **Height** to 7", the **Resolution** to 300 pixels, and the background to transparent.

STEP 5: Use the **View** menu to turn on the rulers and the grid. To set the grid subdivision size, open the **Edit** menu, point to **Preferences**, click **Grid**, and set the **Subdivisions** to 4.

STEP 6: From the **Edit** menu, click **Paste**. The merged persimmon bookplate appears in your new document.

STEP 7: Next, you'll copy and make two smaller sizes of this bookplate. First, make sure the persimmon bookplate's layer is selected.

STEP 8: In the **Layers** palette, click the **MORE** arrow and select **Duplicate Layer**.

STEP 9: Give the new layer a name and click **OK**.

STEP 10: Select the duplicate layer in the **Layers** palette.

STEP 11: From the **Image** menu, point to **Transform**, then click **Free Transform**.

STEP 12: In the options bar, make sure the **Constrain Proportions** button is checked. Then right-click inside the width box (labeled **W**) and select percent from the drop-down list of units.

STEP 13: Change the width to 75%. (Don't worry about the height; it will automatically change to match the width.)

STEP 14: Click the **Commit** checkmark.

STEP 15: Repeat steps 7 through 14, this time changing the width to 50%.

STEP 16: Use the **Move** tool to move the bookplates into the upper left corner of the

document, so there will be more room for additional bookplates. (Remember to select each bookplate's layer before trying to move it.)

STEP 17: Now you'll repeat steps 1 through 16 to copy the other bookplates into the document.

When you're finished, you should have twelve bookplates—three sizes in each of the four colors. **1**

STEP 18: From the **File** menu, click **Save As**, then specify the PNG file format. Saving this file as a PNG file will preserve the transparency around the bookplates. This PNG file will be the file you open to use these bookplates in future scrapbook projects.

Congratulations! You've created a beautiful set of coordinated bookplates. Feel free to experiment with more sizes and colors, and save each set as a PNG file to use later.

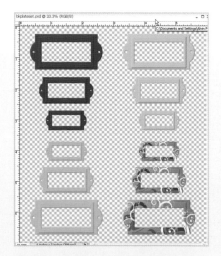

1 The finished document should contain all twelve bookplates.

When you're finished, save and close both your PNG file and your master PSD file. (Remember, you'll still have a bookplate template on the CD with the original bookplate on it, should you need it.)

CREATING DIGITAL TAGS FROM A TEMPLATE

The last template you'll modify in this lesson is a tag template. There are two tag templates in the kit, but you'll only use one in this exercise. You can use the other template later, on your own.

This exercise uses the same steps and techniques you've already learned. It will reinforce your skills and give you a little more practice, while helping you create a gorgeous set of coordinated tags for your scrapbooking projects.

The tag template has three layers that are different colors. You'll add a decorative background to the large section, then you'll recolor the tag's frame, and finally you'll recolor the trim around the hole.

STEP 1: Open the file *dds2ovaltag.psd* from the *templates* folder on the CD that came with this book. ❶

STEP 2: Before you modify the tag, save this file with a different filename (PSD format) to your hard disk so that you can always return to the original if you need to.

STEP 3: Select the bottom *tag shape* layer. ❷

STEP 4: Open the *swooshyswirly8.jpg* file from the backgrounds folder on the CD.

STEP 5: From the **Image** menu, point to **Resize**, then click **Image Size**. Make sure the **Resample Image** box is checked, then set both the width and height to 4" (so it's closer to the size of the tag template document). Then click **OK**.

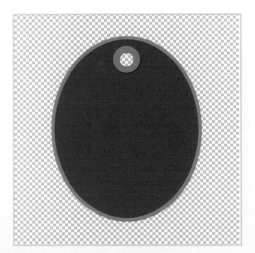

❶ Open the tag template file *dds2ovaltag.psd*.

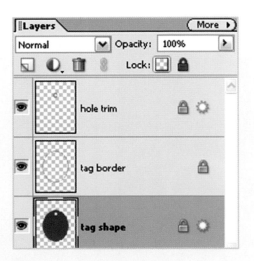

❷ The tag template has three layers.

STEP 6: From the **Select** menu, click **All** to select the entire background.

STEP 7: Copy the background, close the background file, then paste the background into the tag template document. ❸ ❹

STEP 8: Select the decorative layer, then press **CTRL** (**CMD** on a **Mac**) and click inside the *tag shape* layer's thumbnail in the **Layers** palette.

STEP 9: From the **Select** menu, click **Inverse**. Then from the **Edit** menu, click **Cut**.

STEP 10: Because you resized the background file to 4 x 4, some of that pasted background is outside the boundaries of the tag document (which is only 2 x 4). To remove that excess, select **All** from the **Select** menu. Then from the **Image** menu, click **Crop**. Then press **ESC** to remove the selection marquee.

STEP 11: The *tag shape* layer has a **Drop Shadow** Layer Style. To apply the same Layer Style to your decorative layer, press **ALT** while dragging the **Styles** icon from the tag shape layer to the new decorative layer. ❺

STEP 12: Next, you'll change the color of the frame and the trim surrounding the hole. To do this, you first need to change the Foreground color. In previous exercises, you selected the Foreground color from the **Color Swatches** palette. This time, you'll use the **Eyedropper** tool to sample a color from inside your tag's decorative background. First, select the **Eyedropper** tool from the toolbox. Then click inside one of the tiny green dots in the background design. You may need to zoom in to do this. ❻

❸ Paste the decorative background into the tag template.

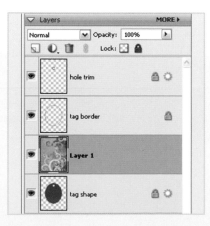

❹ The decorative layer should be just above the tag shape layer.

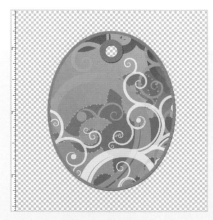

❺ Copy the **Drop Shadow** Layer Style from the *tag shape* layer to the new decorative layer.

The **Eyedropper** tool lets you select a particular shade from another element, instead of being restricted to the swatches in a palette.

STEP 13: Select the *tag border* layer, then from the Edit menu, click **Fill Layer** and choose **Foreground color**.

STEP 14: Change the color of the hole's trim the same way: select the *hole trim* layer, then fill it with the same Foreground color. ❼

Now you have a completed tag! You can continue to make more tags in different colors by following the same steps you used to make additional bookplates. When you are finished, copy your tags to a new 6 x 7 blank file, make additional sizes if you like, and save them as a collection in a PNG file. Need a refresher on how to do all that? Just follow the steps under "Creating a New Bookplates

PNG Document." The steps are exactly the same for this tag, since you're using multiple layers to create a single tag.

Remember, there's a second tag template on the CD, too, so you may want to make additional tags in coordinating colors using that shape, as well.

When you're finished, save and close your PSD master files, as well as your PNG files.

Congratulations! Now you're ready to learn how to create your own embellishments "from scratch"— without using a pre-made template.

❻ Use the **Eyedropper** tool to select the green from the decorative background.

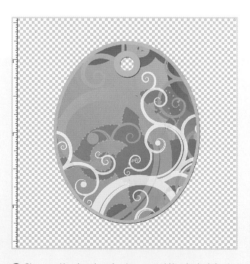

❼ Change the *tag border* layer and the *hole trim* layer to green

create embellishments from scratch

In lesson 1 of this chapter, you learned how to make some of the most versatile digital elements—brads, bookplates, and tags—by modifying templates I created for you. Sometimes, however, you may want to create an embellishment yourself. Two popular embellishments are conchos (metallic rings with prongs on the back that stick them to the page) and metallic disks that are used like bookplates. In this lesson, you'll learn how to create both "from scratch."

The exercises in this lesson will show you how to add and remove shadows, as well as how to use filters, layer style effects, and other tools to change the appearance of a shape. You'll be amazed at how realistic your embellishments will look! (And don't be surprised if people touch your pages to see if the embellishments are "real"!)

CREATING THE BASIC CONCHO SHAPE

The Bevel Layer Style will give depth to your conchos. The following steps show how.

STEP 1: Open Photoshop Elements and go to the Editor workspace.

STEP 2: Create a new blank file and name it *concho*. Set the **Width** and **Height** to 1", the **Resolution** to 300 pixels, the color mode to RGB Color, and the background to white.

STEP 3: Use the **View** menu to turn on the rulers, the grid, and **Snap to Grid**. Then open the **Edit** menu, point to **Preferences**, click **Grid**, and set the **Subdivisions** to 16.

STEP 4: Click the **Create a new layer** button and name the layer *concho*.

STEP 5: For this step you'll use the **Elliptical Marquee** tool. Chances are your toolbox shows the **Rectangular Marquee** tool, because that's the last marquee tool we used. To find the **Elliptical Marquee** tool, first click the **Rectangular Marquee** icon, and then select the **Elliptical Marquee** tool from the options bar. ❶

❶ TECH TIP

See the little triangle at the bottom right corner of some of the tool icons in the toolbox? If you right-click that little triangle, all the variations of that tool appear in a drop-down list, and you can select one from the list. The same variations of the tool are also displayed in the tool's options bar.

STEP 6: Use the **Elliptical Marquee** tool to draw a ½" circular marquee in the middle of your document (in the new layer you just created). The easiest way to do this is to specify its measurements in the options bar. Set **Feather** to **0 px** and make sure **Anti-alias** is checked. **Set Mode** to **Fixed Size**. Then set both the **Width**

❶ Choose the **Elliptical Marquee** tool from the options bar.

ℹ INFO TIP

When creating a new embellishment, I usually choose a white background when I need to see what the finished image will look like. Sometimes you can't see that without some kind of background, and white is the simplest to use. I turn off the white background's visibility when it's time to save the element as a PNG file, so that the background then becomes transparent.

and the **Height** to **0.5 in**. When you have all the measurements set in the options bar, click once inside your document and the marquee will appear in the correct size. Then move the selection marquee to the center of your document. ❷

ℹ️ **TECH TIP**

In Chapter 1, when you created your background pattern of tiny circles, you used the **Shape Tool** to draw the circles. In this lesson, you'll use the **Elliptical Marquee** tool to draw a circle because you'll be altering this shape in the coming steps.

You've probably discovered by now that there are often several ways to complete a single task in Photoshop Elements. This gives you powerful flexibility, but it can be confusing if you're learning for the first time. The good news is that as you become more proficient with the software, you'll settle on your favorite ways to do things. In this book, I've tried to show you at least some of the options you're most likely to use.

STEP 7: Click the **Paint Bucket** tool. Then select **lime** from the **Color Swatches** palette and click once inside your circle to fill it with lime. ❸

STEP 8: Turn off the selection marquee by pressing **ESC**.

STEP 9: Select the **Elliptical Marquee** tool again. This time, change both the **Width** and the **Height** to **0.45 in**, then click inside your document. Then move the selection marquee to the center of your lime circle. ❹

STEP 10: Press **DEL** to delete the selected inner portion of the lime circle. ❺

STEP 11: Turn off the selection marquee by pressing **ESC**.

That's it for the basic concho shape. Now you can give it depth and realism.

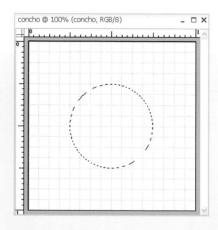

❷ Draw an elliptical marquee in the center of the document.

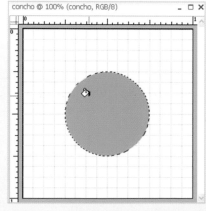

❸ Use the **Paint Bucket** tool to fill the circle with lime.

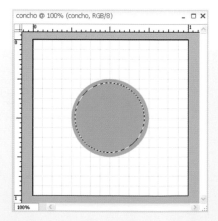

❹ Move the new elliptical selection marquee to the center of the lime circle.

STEP 12: From the **Palette Bin**, open the **Artwork and Effects** palette. Then click the **Apply Effects, Filters and Layer Styles** button. A gallery of special effects appears.* **6**

STEP 13: From the **Select a category** drop-down list, choose **Layer Styles**. In the **View a subcategory** drop-down list, choose **Bevels**.*

*Note: If you're using Adobe Photoshop Elements 4.0, open the **Styles and Effects** palette, then choose **Layer Styles** and **Bevels** in the drop-down lists.

STEP 14: Click the **Simple Emboss** layer style, then click the **Apply** button at the bottom of the palette. (In Photoshop Elements 4.0, you don't need to click **Apply**. Just clicking the layer style will apply it to your selected layer.) **7**

Just that quickly, you have a concho! But you're not finished yet. I don't like the shadowing very much—it's too computer-like. I'd rather create my own. So let's do that now.

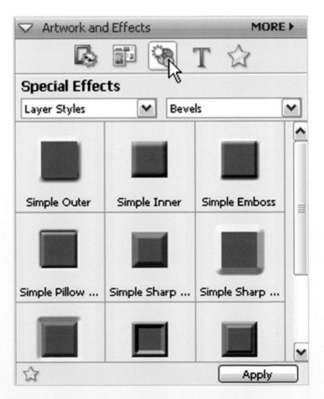

5 Press **DEL** to delete the inner circle.

6 Click the **Apply Effects, Filters and Layer Styles button.**

CREATE YOUR OWN SHADOW

To replace the shadow, first you must remove the existing one, then create a new one. I'll show you two ways to do this. First, we'll create a shadow using the drop shadow layer style. Then we'll create a drop shadow from scratch.

ⓓ DESIGN TIP

When I'm creating digital elements to use in future layouts, I generally don't apply a shadow. Or if I do, I make sure it's a very small shadow. That way I have the flexibility to add an appropriate shadow when I place the element in my layout. The choice is yours and will depend upon the element you're designing.

STEP 1: Select the concho's shape by pressing **CTRL** (**CMD** on a **Mac**) and clicking inside the concho layer's thumbnail in the **Layers** palette. ❶

STEP 2: Because the area you want to delete is outside the concho itself, you need to reverse the selection. From the **Select** menu, click **Inverse**. But don't delete it yet!

STEP 3: Before you delete the shadow, there is something you must do to the layer. So first save this selection in case you accidentally turn it off it during the next step. To save the selection, open the **Select** menu and click **Save Selection**, then name it *shadow*.

STEP 4: Now you need to simplify the layer. Click **MORE** at the top right corner of the **Layers** palette, then click **Simplify Layer**. ❷

ⓣ TECH TIP

Photoshop Elements lets you simplify layers that have elements in them such as shapes (your concho) or type. Simplifying a layer turns it into an image layer. One benefit of turning shape

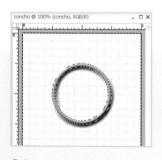

❶ Select the concho's shape.

❷ Simplify the layer.

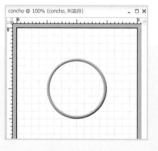

❸ Press **DEL** to remove the selected shadow area of the layer.

❹ If you accidentally turned off the selection marquee, you can reload it.

layers into image layers is that it reduces the size of the file. Another benefit is that you can only apply filters to image layers.

STEP 5: Now that the layer is simplified, you can remove the portions of the layer you don't want—the shadow. If your inverted selection is still active, press **DEL** to remove the shadow. ❸

If you accidentally turned off the selection marquee before you could delete the shadow, retrieve the selection by opening the **Select** menu and clicking **Load Selection**. Select *shadow* and the selection marquee will reappear. Now you can press **DEL** to remove the shadow area. ❹

STEP 6: Turn off the selection marquee by pressing **ESC**.

STEP 7: In the **Artwork and Effects** palette (or **Styles and Effects** in Photoshop Elements 4.0),

open the **View a subcategory** drop-down list and select **Drop Shadows**. Then click the **Low** drop shadow and apply it to your layer. ❺ ❻

I'm still not happy with the shadow effect, but this time I can adjust it.

STEP 8: Double-click the **Styles** icon, located to the right of the concho layer's name in the **Layers** palette. ❼ In the **Styles Settings** dialog box that appears, change the **Size** to **8 px** and change the **Distance** to **3 px**. Then click **OK**. ❽ That's much better!

If you are using Photoshop Elements 4.0, you can only change the size of the shadow, but not the distance. That makes your shadow appear a little further away than the shadow in the example. Sometimes that's okay. But if you're not happy with it, you can always create a drop shadow from scratch, as the following steps explain.

❺ Select the **Low** drop shadow layer style.

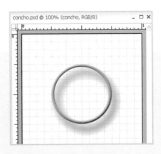

❻ The concho appears with a **Low** drop shadow.

❼ Click the **Styles** icon in the concho layer.

❽ Adjust the size and distance of the shadow style.

CREATE A DROP SHADOW FROM SCRATCH

This technique will work for both Photoshop Elements 4.0 and 5.0. First, you'll duplicate your concho layer, and then you'll modify the duplicate layer so that you don't lose what you've done so far with the original layer.

ⓓ DESIGN TIP

"Back in the day" when Photoshop didn't have Layer Styles, I had to make my own shadows from scratch. I still use this technique often because it's simple and gives me maximum control of a shadow's look and position.

STEP 1: To duplicate the layer, click **MORE** in the **Layers** palette and click **Duplicate Layer**.

STEP 2: Turn off the visibility of the original concho layer by clicking its eye icon. ❶

STEP 3: Select the *new concho copy* layer.

STEP 4: To remove the drop shadow layer style, click **MORE** in the **Layers** palette and click **Clear Layer Style**. ❷

STEP 5: Click the **Create a new layer** button, name it *shadow*, and drag it so that it is below the duplicated layer in the **Layers** palette.

STEP 6: Make sure the *shadow* layer is selected. Then select the duplicated concho's shape by pressing **CTRL** (**CMD** on a **Mac**) and clicking inside the *concho copy* layer's thumbnail. ❸

STEP 7: To fill the selected area of the shadow layer with black, open the **Edit** menu, point to **Fill Selection**, and for **Use**: choose **Black**. (That way you don't have to change the foreground color.)

STEP 8: To remove the selection marquee, press **ESC**.

STEP 9: Now you'll use the Gaussian Blur filter to blur the shadow. Make sure the *shadow* layer is

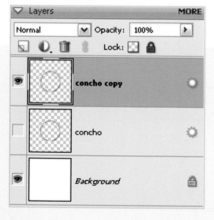

❶ Duplicate the concho layer and turn off the original concho layer's visibility.

❷ Clear the drop shadow layer style from the duplicated layer.

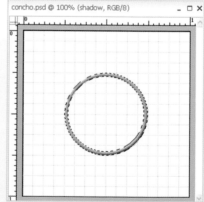

❸ With the *shadow* layer selected, select the concho shape.

still selected. From the **Filter** menu, point to **Blur**, then click **Gaussian Blur**. In the dialog box that appears, set the **Radius** to 3 pixels. ❹

ℹ TECH TIP

The Gaussian Blur filter blurs a selection by an adjustable amount. Because it produces a hazy effect, it's perfect for creating shadows.

STEP 10: Select the **Move** tool, then use the **ARROW** keys to nudge the shadow three taps down and three taps to the right.

STEP 11: I like this shadow, but if it's too dark for you, just adjust the *shadow* layer's opacity until you're satisfied. That's the beauty of this technique—you can adjust the shadow until it's exactly what you want. In fact, with this technique, you can even change your shadow's color.

STEP 12: Turn off the grid and select a different tool (such as the **Hand** tool) to get rid of the **Move** tool's bounding box, and then admire your new concho! ❺

STEP 13: Turn off the visibility of the *background* layer.

STEP 14: Save your document as a PNG file.

STEP 15: Now create a collection of conchos using the other colors in the Lolly color palette and smaller sizes to match the other elements you've already created.

Now that you know how to create your own shadows, you'll have even more creative control over your elements!

And here's even better news: creating an eyelet is just as simple as creating a concho. Just start with a smaller circle (¼" in width and height), make the center hole smaller (0.08 inches), and adjust the bevel size to 35 pixels. Try it now, using the same steps you used to make a concho! ❻

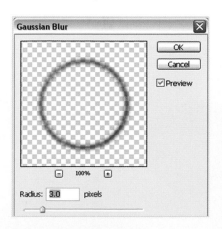

❹ Set the **Gaussian Blur** filter's radius to 3 pixels.

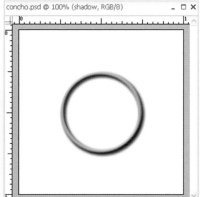

❺ Use the **ARROW** keys to nudge the shadow three space down and three space to the right.

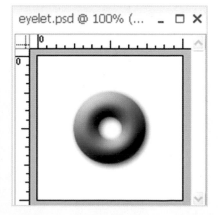

❻ Use the same steps to create an eyelet.

CREATING A METALLIC DISK
BOOKPLATE FROM SCRATCH

By now, you've probably figured out how I created the bookplate template you modified in the last chapter. I constructed it using geometric shapes on separate layers with bevel layer styles applied to each layer.

Since you're already familiar with the bevel style, you can construct your own multi-layered elements now. Let's try making a round bookplate. And to make this disk even more interesting, we'll give it a metallic finish.

CREATE THE BASE LAYERS

STEP 1: Create a new blank file and name it *disk*. Set the **Width** and **Height** to 1", the **Resolution** to 300 pixels, the color mode to RGB Color, and the background to white.

STEP 2: Use the **View** menu to turn on the rulers, the grid, and **Snap to Grid**. Then open the **Edit** menu, point to **Preferences**, click **Grid**, and set the **Subdivisions** to 16.

STEP 3: Click the **Create a new** layer button and name the new layer *base*.

STEP 4: Return the foreground and background color boxes in the toolbox to their default black and white. To do this, click the tiny black and white box in the corner of the color boxes icon.

STEP 5: Click the **Elliptical Marquee** tool. Set **Feather** to **0 px** and make sure **Anti-alias** is checked. Set **Mode** to **Fixed Size**. Then set both the **Width** and the **Height** to **0.5 in**.

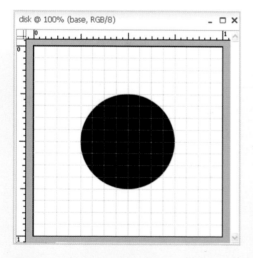

❶ Draw an elliptical marquee in the center of the document.

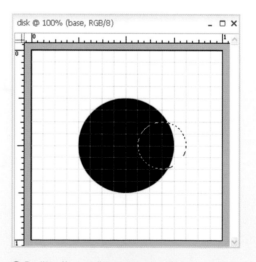

❷ Position the smaller marquee so it overlaps the right side of the base circle.

STEP 6: Click once inside your document to make the elliptical marquee appear, then move the selection marquee to the center of your document. **1**

STEP 7: Fill the selected circle with **black**.

STEP 8: To create the two tabs on the sides of the bookplate, you'll again use the **Elliptical Marquee** tool. This time, set the width and height to **0.25 in**.

STEP 9: Click inside the document once. Position the selection marquee so that part of it overlaps the right side of the base circle. **2**

STEP 10: Fill the smaller circle with **black**. **3**

STEP 11: To create a second circle, move the same selection marquee to the left side of the base layer and again fill it with **black**. **4**

STEP 12: Remove the selection marquee by pressing **ESC**.

Now the base layer is complete. Next, you'll duplicate this layer and then make the duplicate a little smaller.

STEP 13: With the *base* layer selected, click **MORE** at the top of the **Layers** palette and click **Duplicate Layer**.

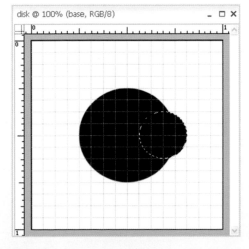

3 Fill the smaller circle with black.

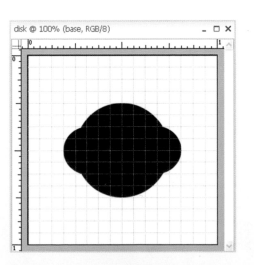

4 Move the selection marquee to the left side of the base circle and again fill it with black.

71

STEP 14: With the new duplicate layer selected, press **CTRL** (**CMD** on a **Mac**) and click inside the shape's thumbnail in the Layers palette. When the shape is selected, fill it with the **Background color** (white). ❺

ℹ️ INFO TIP

When designing a multi-layered, beveled embellishment, I recommend making each layer a different color so it's easier to see them and avoid confusion. When you finish creating the layers, you can go back and apply the correct colors to each layer for your finished look.

STEP 15: Now make this layer slightly smaller. To do this, open the **Image** menu, point to **Resize**, then click **Scale**. In the options bar, make sure **Constrain Proportions** is checked, then set either the width or the height to 95% (the other dimension will adjust automatically). ❻ Then click **Commit**. ❼

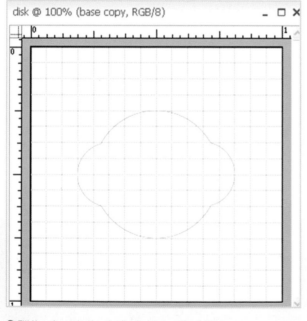

❺ Fill the shape in the duplicate layer with white.

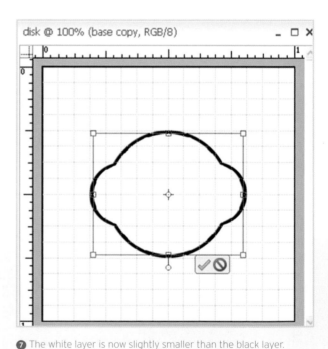

❼ The white layer is now slightly smaller than the black layer.

❻ Change the width and height of the *base copy* layer to 95%.

MAKE HOLES IN THE LAYERS

You'll use the **Elliptical Marquee** tool again to make holes in the tabs.

STEP 1: Click the **Elliptical Marquee** tool, and set the width and height to **0.05 in**.

STEP 2: Click inside the document, and position the small circle over the *base copy* layer's right-hand tab.

STEP 3: Press **DEL**, and the small circle of the white layer will be deleted, letting black show through. ❶

STEP 4: Select the *base* layer in the **Layers** palette, and then press **DEL** again. That will delete the circle from the black layer.

STEP 5: Move the selection marquee to the left side of the image and create a hole through both layers there, too.

STEP 6: To make sure the holes go through both layers, turn off the visibility of the *background* layer. You should be able to see the checkerboard background through the holes. ❷

STEP 7: Lock the transparent pixels of both the *base* layer and the *base copy* layer. (Select a layer, then click the **Lock transparent pixels** button in the **Layers** palette.) ❸

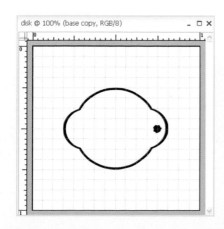

❶ Delete a hole (circle) from the *base copy* layer.

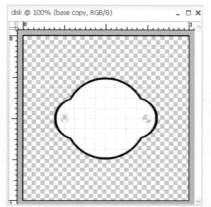

❷ Turn off the background layer's visibility to ensure the holes go through both layers.

❸ Lock the transparent pixels in both the *base* layer and the *base copy* layer.

STEP 8: Now you'll remove the center sections. With the **Elliptical Marquee** tool selected, set the width and height to **0.4 in**.

STEP 9: Click once inside the document, then position the selection marquee in the center of your embellishment. ❹

STEP 10: Delete this circle from both the *base* and the *base copy* layers, the same way you deleted the holes. ❺

STEP 11: Remove the selection marquee by pressing **ESC**.

Your round bookplate is nearly finished. Shall we make it look metallic now?

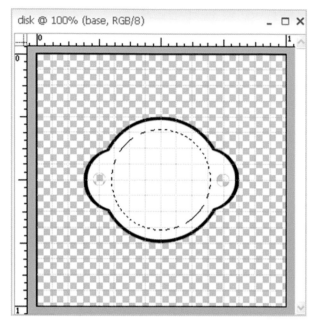

❹ Position the new selection marquee in the center of the disk.

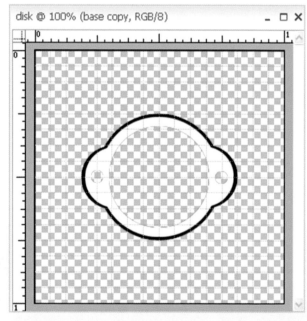

❺ Delete a circle from both the *base* layer and the *base copy* layer.

ADD A METALLIC FINISH

It's time to make your round bookplate look real. First, you'll add a metallic finish to both layers by using the **Linear Gradient** tool. Then you'll add bevels and a drop shadow to give it depth.

STEP 1: Select the **Gradient** tool. ▣ The options bar displays several variations of the **Gradient** tool. Make sure you've selected the **Linear Gradient** tool. This variation applies the gradient from the starting point to the ending point in a straight line.

❶ TECH TIP
The **Gradient** tool creates a gradual blend between multiple colors. You can choose from preset gradient fills or create your own. You fill an area with a gradient by dragging in the image. The starting point (where you first click your mouse) and ending point (where you release the mouse) affect the gradient appearance, depending on the **Gradient** tool you're using. For more information about gradients and the **Gradient** tool, see Adobe Photoshop Elements Help.

STEP 2: In the options bar, click the drop-down arrow to open the **Gradient picker**.

STEP 3: In the **Gradient picker**, click the small arrow button and select **Metals** from the drop-down list. ❶ Five colors of gradients appear in the **Gradient picker**.

STEP 4: Click the **Silver** gradient (position the cursor over each gradient to see its name).

STEP 5: Turn off the *base copy* layer's visibility.

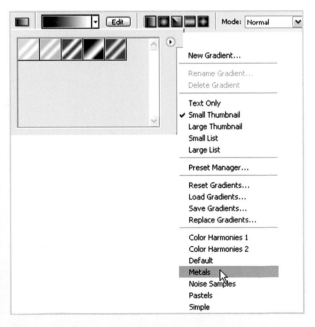

❶ Select **Metals** from the **Gradient** list.

STEP 6: Select the *base* layer. Position the cursor in the top left corner of your document. Click and hold the mouse button down as you drag to the lower right corner of the document, then release the mouse. ❷ The gradient is applied to the layer. ❸

ⓣ **TECH TIP**

Where you position your cursor as you draw the gradient line will determine how the gradient is applied to your image. You can achieve a variety of different effects simply by applying the gradient from different start and end points. I chose to use a diagonal line in this project so the silver gradient will appear more realistic.

STEP 7: Now you can apply the bevel style to this layer. To do this, use the **Artwork and Effects** palette (**Styles and Effects** palette in Photoshop Elements 4.0), choose **Bevels** from the **View a subcategory** list, click the **Simple Inner** layer style, and click **Apply**.

STEP 8: Double-click the **Styles** icon beside the *base* layer's name in the **Layers** palette. In the **Styles Settings** dialog box that appears, change the **Size** to **2 px**. Then click **OK**. ❹

STEP 9: Turn on the *base copy* layer's visibility.

STEP 10: Select the *base copy* layer and apply the same gradient to this layer using the same positions as in Step 6.

STEP 11: Now you can copy the bevel style to this layer. First, select the *base* layer. Then, from the **Layer** menu, point to **Layer Style**, then click **Copy Layer Style**.

STEP 12: Now select the *base copy* layer. Then, from the **Layer** menu, point to **Layer Style**, then click **Paste Layer Style**. ❺

Next, you'll create drop shadow.

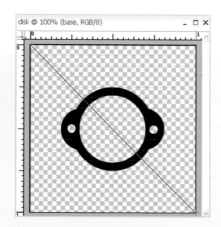

❷ Click and drag from the upper left corner to the lower right corner of the *base* layer.

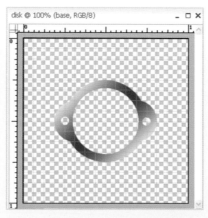

❸ The gradient is applied to the layer.

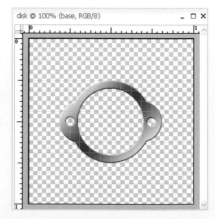

❹ Apply the **Simple Inner** bevel style and change its size to 2 pixels.

STEP 13: Click the **Create a new layer** button and name the new layer *shadow*. Then drag the new layer to the bottom of the **Layers** palette (just above the background layer).

STEP 14: Keeping the *shadow* layer selected, press **CTRL** (**CMD** on a **Mac**) and click inside the *base* layer's thumbnail.

STEP 15: Fill the selection with **black**.

STEP 16: Add a **Gaussian Blur** filter by opening the **Filter** menu, pointing to **Blur**, then clicking **Gaussian Blur**. Set the **Radius** to **3 pixels**, then click **OK**.

STEP 17: Click the **Move** tool, then use the **ARROW** keys to nudge the shadow one space to the right and one space down. ❻

STEP 18: Turn off the grid to see your new embellishment!

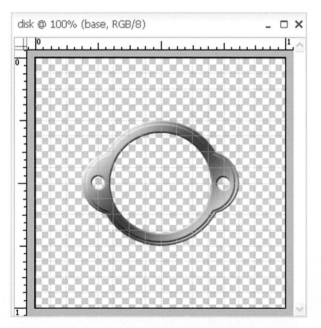

❺ Paste the bevel layer style onto the *base copy* layer.

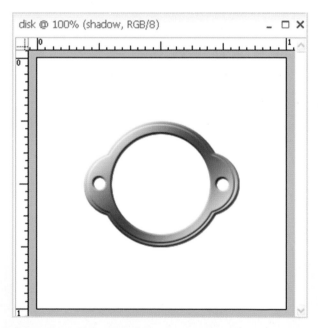

❻ The finished round bookplate.

STEP 19: Make sure the background layer's visibility is still turned off, then save the file in PNG format to preserve the transparency around the bookplate.

STEP 20: Save the file as a PSD file, too, so that you can use it later to make additional bookplates in other colors or sizes.

That's it! You've created your own concho and bookplate from scratch. You've learned about bevels, shadows, and gradients, and you've found out that just because a digital element looks complicated doesn't mean it is.

Now you're ready for the last lesson in this chapter: how to make digital chipboard!

create digital chipboard

It seems chipboard is everywhere in scrapbook layouts these days—chipboard letters, chipboard decorations, chipboard backgrounds... You'll be pleased to know that digital chipboard is wonderfully easy to create.

This last lesson is a short one, because you've already learned all the skills you need. So instead of learning a new technique, you'll learn how to apply what you already know in new ways to create yet another realistic-looking, tremendously versatile embellishment—chipboard letters.

CREATING A CHIPBOARD LETTER

By the time you're finished with this lesson, you'll be well on your way to creating a whole alphabet of those large chipboard letters that are so popular right now.

STEP 1: Open Photoshop Elements and go to the Editor workspace.

STEP 2: Create a new blank file and name it *alphachip*. Set the **Width** and **Height** to 3", the **Resolution** to 300 pixels, the color mode to RGB Color, and the background to transparent.

STEP 3: Let's start by placing a digital background from the CD into your new document. From the **File** menu, click **Place**. Then navigate to the *swooshygreen8.jpg* file in the *backgrounds* folder on the CD. Click **Place**. The artwork from the background file appears inside a bounding box at the center of your document. ❶

STEP 4: Click **Commit**.

STEP 5: Click the **Horizontal Type** tool, and select a font. I used **Georgia Regular**. The color and size don't matter at this stage.

STEP 6: Type an uppercase **A**. ❷

STEP 7: Change the font size until the letter is approximately 2" tall. I used 208 points, but you may need to adjust up or down depending on the font you use.

STEP 8: Use the **Move** tool to position the letter so it covers the portion of the background you want to apply to the letter shape. ❸

STEP 9: Turn off the *type* layer's visibility.

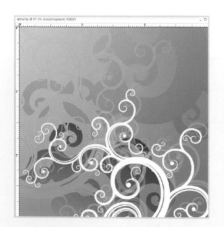

❶ **Place** the *swooshygreen8.jpg* file into your document.

❷ Use the **Horizontal Type** tool to type an uppercase **A**.

❸ Enlarge the letter A and position it over the portion of the background you want to appear on the letter.

STEP 10: Select the background layer. Then press **CTRL** (**CMD** on a **Mac**) and click inside the letter's thumbnail in the **Layers** palette. ❹

STEP 11: Because you want to remove all of the background outside the letter, open the **Select** menu and click **Inverse**.

STEP 12: Press **DEL** to delete the extraneous background, then press **ESC** to turn off the selection marquee. ❺

STEP 13: Now you can apply a bevel style. Open the **Artworks and Effects palette** (**Styles and Effects** in Photoshop Elements 4.0) and select the **Layer Styles** category and the **Bevels** subcategory. Then apply the **Simple Inner** bevel style. ❻

STEP 14: Double-click the **Styles** icon for the background layer. In the **Style Settings** dialog box, adjust the **Size** until you're satisfied. I used **12** pixels. ❼

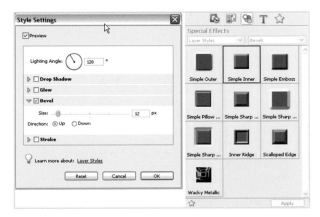

❼ Adjust the size of the bevel.

❹ Select the background layer and then select the letter's shape.

❺ Delete the extraneous background.

❻ Click the **Styles** icon in the concho layer.

STEP 15: You can add more than one layer style to a layer. Let's add a drop shadow to the letter. Select the **Drop Shadows** subcategory, then select **Low**. Double-click the **Styles** icon again, and this time change the drop shadow's **Size** to **3 px**, the **Distance** to **3 px**, and the **Opacity** to **75%**. (If you're using Photoshop Elements 4.0, you won't be able to adjust the distance.) **8**

STEP 16: Use the **Move** tool to center the letter in the document. **9**

STEP 17: Save this letter as a PNG file to preserve the transparency around it. Name it *alphachip-a.png*.

Why did we give the PNG file a unique name? Because you're going to create a complete set of chipboard letters, saving each one as an individual PNG file! Or, you can create a larger document to contain your entire alphabet set, like I did with the set on the CD. You learned how to do this with the other digital elements. Just follow the same steps.

CREATING A SECOND CHIPBOARD LETTER

Now let's make a second letter—this time, a B. You'll continue to build this letter in the same master PSD file you used to create the A. However, you'll use a different background this time, just for variety.

STEP 1: Turn off the original *swooshygreen8* layer's visibility.

STEP 2: From the **File** menu, click **Place**, and locate the *swooshyorange8.jpg* background file on the CD. Place it into your document. **1**

STEP 3: Turn the *A* layer's visibility back on.

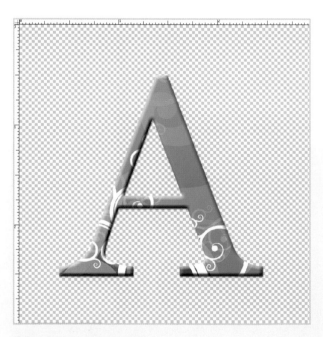

9 The finished chipboard letter.

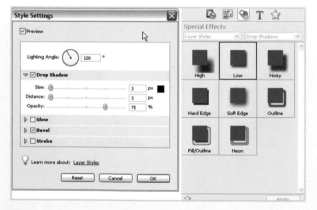

8 Add a drop shadow and adjust its size, distance, and opacity.

STEP 4: Double-click the *A* layer's thumbnail in the **Layers** palette, then change the letter from an A to a B. (Double-clicking the thumbnail selects the letter, so when you type a B, the A is replaced.) ❷

STEP 5: Use the **Move** tool to position the letter over the background.

STEP 6: Turn off the *type* layer's visibility.

STEP 7: Select the background layer. Then press **CTRL** (**CMD** on a **Mac**) and click inside the letter's thumbnail in the **Layers** palette.

STEP 8: From the **Select** menu, click **Inverse**, then press **DEL**. Press **ESC** to turn off the selection marquee.

STEP 9: Now, instead of applying a new bevel style and drop shadow to the letter B, you can simply copy the layer styles from the A you already created. Press **ALT** and drag the **Styles** icon from the A layer (*swooshygreen8*) to the B layer (*swooshyorange8*) in the **Layers** palette.

STEP 10: Use the **Move** tool to center the letter in the document. ❸

STEP 11: Save this letter as a PNG file named *alphachip-b.png*.

❶ Place the *v* file in your document.

❷ Replace the A with a B.

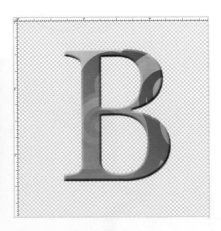

❸ The finished chipboard letter.

Now you know everything you need to complete your set of digital chipboard alphabets! Chipboard letters are a fun way to liven up a layout. Here are some tips to think about while you're creating your letters:

- Try using different backgrounds or the same background from different angles so that each letter is unique. Mix in some with solid colors, too.
- Remember to create numbers and punctuation marks, too. Chipboard brackets make great page embellishments.
- Try out lots of fonts to see what interesting embellishments you can make. Picture fonts (sometimes called dingbats) can make some inventive and artistic digital elements.

Congratulations on adding a whole range of embellishments to your digital arsenal. You've learned how to customize digital elements from a template, how to create your own elements from scratch, and how to make an entire alphabet of chipboard letters.

Now that you've mastered all of that, are you ready to tackle some special effects? Then you're ready for the next chapter.

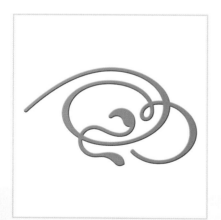
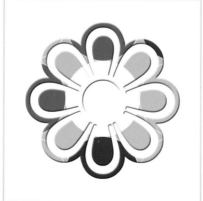

Here are a few examples of the kinds of chipboard elements you can make.

using brushes
& other special effects

One of the most versatile tools in Photoshop Elements is the **Brush** tool. As its name implies, it certainly can be used like paint brushes in the real world, to add color to your images. But one of the most interesting ways to use brushes is to treat them as digital rubber stamps.

In the first lesson of this chapter, you'll learn how brushes work in Photoshop Elements and some of the ways you can use them. In the second lesson, you'll download brushes I've provided for you on the CD, and then use them like rubber stamps. The third lesson will show you how to create your own digital brushes. And the final lesson will show you a few of my favorite tips and tricks!

ⓣ TECH TIP

If you have a pen tablet (also called a digitizing tablet), you're a very lucky duck because pen tablets are the perfect tools to use with brushes. If you have one, simply use it instead of your mouse for the brush lessons.

understanding brushes

Although this chapter isn't about digital painting, before you can start to use brushes confidently, it helps to understand some basic concepts and techniques. So let's start by exploring the default brushes that come with Photoshop Elements. These brushes, with their settings already determined, are called **Presets**. You can use the preset brushes as they are, or you can modify and customize them as needed.

In this lesson, you'll create a sample file and play around with some brushes, just to get comfortable with them. Then you'll use brushes to "colorize" a black-and-white photo!

EXPERIMENTING WITH THE BRUSH TOOL

Let's create a sample file and begin experimenting with brushes.

STEP 1: Open Photoshop Elements and go to the Editor workspace.

STEP 2: Create a new blank file named *brushsamples*. Set both the **Width** and **Height** to 6", the **Resolution** to 300 pixels, the **Color Mode** to RGB Color, and the **Background Contents** to White. Don't turn on the grid for this exercise.

STEP 3: Click the **Create a new layer** button and name it *soft round 13*. ❶ This refers to the type of brush you'll use first: a soft-bristled, round brush with a diameter of 13 pixels.

STEP 4: Reset the **Foreground** and **Background** colors to their default black and white. To do this,

you can either click the tiny black and white boxes next to the color boxes in the toolbox, or you can press the lowercase D on your keyboard.

STEP 5: Click the **Brush** tool ✎ in the toolbox. If you've used Photoshop Elements' brushes before, the settings in the options bar will be what you used last time. Let's reset the settings to their defaults to make sure your settings match the examples in this exercise. To do this, click the **Brush** tool icon at the left of the options bar and select **Reset Tool**. ❷

STEP 6: In the options bar, click the arrow beside the sample brush to display the **Brush Preset** palette.

STEP 7: In the palette's **Brushes** box, make sure **Default Brushes** is selected. ❸ Then press **ENTER** to close the **Brush Preset** palette.

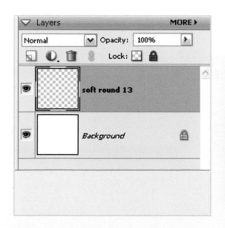

❶ Create a new layer named *soft round 13*.

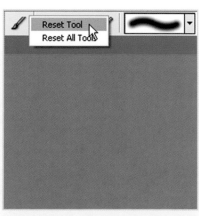

❷ Reset the **Brush** tool to its default settings.

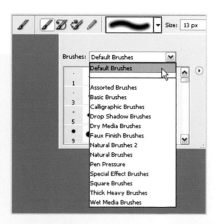

❸ Select **Default Brushes.**

The default preset is a soft brush that's 13 pixels in size. But if you scroll down, you'll see a variety of presets to choose from—both in hardness and in brush size (in pixels). The maximum brush size is 2500 pixels. This is important to remember, because it will make a difference when you start to create your own brushes. (But don't worry, I'll remind you!)

STEP 8: Select the *soft round 13* layer. Using the default 13 pixel brush, click and drag to create a brush stroke across your page. You'll notice it's nearly impossible to draw a straight line! So delete this one by opening the **Edit** menu and selecting **Undo Brush Tool**.

STEP 9: This time, press the **SHIFT** key while you click and drag a line across your document to create a straight line. ❹ Another way to create a straight line is to click a starting point, then press **SHIFT** while clicking an end point.

STEP 10: Create a new layer, and name it **hard round 13**.

STEP 11: Now you'll draw a line with a different brush. Open the **Brush Preset** palette again, and this time select the **Hard Round 13 pixels** brush. (To see the brush names, hover the cursor over each one.) ❺

STEP 12: Press **SHIFT** while you click and drag a straight line. ❻

See the difference between the two strokes? While they're both 13 pixels in size, the soft brush yields a more feathery, softer stroke. Sometimes you'll want to use a hard brush, while other times only a soft brush will do.

MODIFYING A BRUSH PRESET

Now you know that brush presets are nothing more than default brush tips that Photoshop Elements provides.

❹ Create a new layer named *soft round 13*.

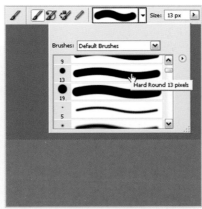

❺ Select the **Hard Round 13 pixels** brush.

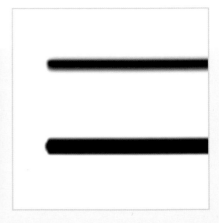

❻ Draw a line with the **Hard Round 13 pixels** brush.

But what if you want to tweak a preset just a little to get the exact brush tip you want? For example, in the default brush set, the soft round brushes are all set to 0% on the Hardness scale, and the hard round brushes are set to 100%. What if you need something in between?

Let's explore some of the **Brush** tool's options that allow you to change a brush's hardness, size, painting mode, and more.

STEP 1: Add a new layer and name it *medium round 13*.

STEP 2: In the **Brush** tool's options bar, click the **More Options** icon. In the dialog box that appears, change the brush **Hardness** to 50%. (You can either use the slider or type in the percentage.) ❶

STEP 3: Press **SHIFT** while you click and drag another straight line. Compare it to the lines you drew earlier.

STEP 4: Add another layer and name it *medium round 25*.

STEP 5: Now let's try increasing the size of this brush. Click the **Size** box in the options bar and change the size to 25 pixels. (You can use the slider or type 25 in the box.) ❷

STEP 6: Now you can change the brush's painting mode. First, add another layer and name it *med round 25 dissolve*.

STEP 7: In the options bar, click the **Mode** box and select **Dissolve** from the drop-down list of **Painting Modes**. ❸ Then draw another line. Notice how this line looks "fuzzy." ❹

❷ Increase the brush size to 25 pixels.

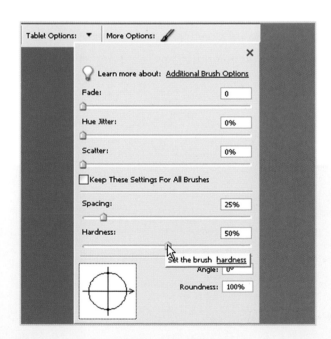

❶ Change the brush hardness to 50%.

❸ Select the Dissolve painting mode.

❹ The **Dissolve** mode makes the line look fuzzy.

Painting modes interact with whatever is on the layer when you begin painting. Because your sample layers are all blank, some of these modes will not yield a result, since there is nothing on the layer to interact with. You'll have a chance later to see how some of the other brush modes work.

STEP 8: Add another new layer and name it *med round 25 opacity 75*. In the options bar, change the painting **Mode** back to **Normal** and then change the **Opacity** to 75%. ❺ Opacity specifies the amount of paint coverage applied to each stroke. Notice how the brush's sample image in the options bar changes as you adjust the opacity. Draw another straight line to see the effect of the opacity setting.

STEP 9: Add another new layer and name it *med round 25 airbrush*. Return the **Opacity** to 100% and then click the **Airbrush** icon ✺ in the options bar. The airbrush feature lets you use the brush to apply gradual tones to an image, simulating traditional airbrush techniques. ❻ Draw another line, but this time, at the end of the stroke, continue to hold down your mouse button. Notice how the paint drop gradually widens and becomes denser, just as if you were using an airbrush. The brush will widen up to the maximum size of the brush tip setting (in this case, 25 pixels).

See how easy it is to adjust brushes to suit your own needs? The next step is to save your new brushes.

So far, you've only used brushes from the **Default Brush** set (called a "library"). But there are many more libraries of brushes to choose from. Spend some time getting to know them. (Open the **Brush Preset** palette, then click in the **Brushes** box to display a list of the different libraries of brush presets. ❼) You'll find brushes in nearly every shape from calligraphy tips to splatters to rubber duckies.

Try different combinations of size, hardness and opacity until you're comfortable playing with the brushes.

When you're finished, close your *brushsamples* document and move on to the next exercise, where you'll get to do a little painting with brushes.

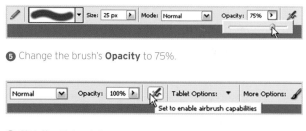

❺ Change the brush's **Opacity** to 75%.

❻ Click the Airbrush icon.

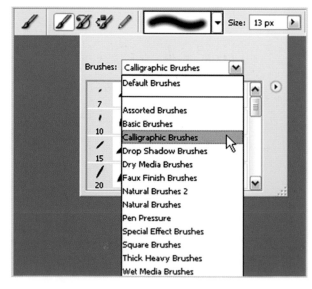

❼ Explore the various brush preset libraries.

USING MORE BRUSH SETTINGS

By now, you should be pretty comfortable using most of the preset brushes. In this exercise, you'll use a variety of brush settings to modify a color photograph.

STEP 1: Reset the brushes to their original settings by clicking the **Brush** tool icon on the left side of the options bar and then clicking **Reset Tool**.

STEP 2: Open the *flowers.jpg* file from the *other* folder on the CD that came with this book. ❶

STEP 3: Duplicate the background layer so you'll have the original photo to go back to if you need it. (Click **More** in the **Layers** palette and click **Duplicate Layer**.)

STEP 4: Open the **Color Swatches** palette and click **persimmon** to set the foreground color.

STEP 5: Select the **Brush** tool and open the **Brush Presets** palette. Select the **Default Brushes** library, then click the **Soft Round 45 pixels** brush.

STEP 6: Paint over one of the petals by clicking and dragging your mouse over the area. ❷ As you can see, without any adjustments the preset brush paints an opaque "coat" over the photograph.

STEP 7: Using the same brush, change its **Opacity** to 35%. Now paint over another petal, making sure you keep the mouse button depressed the entire time. ❸ With the opacity lowered, you can see some of the photograph through the paint.

STEP 8: Now paint over the same petal again with the same brush. ❹ Every time you release the mouse button and then paint again, you're adding another coat of paint, and it becomes more opaque, just as real paint does. If you keep adding coats, eventually you'll hide the petal completely.

❶ Open the *flowers.jpg* file.

❷ Use the brush to paint over one petal.

❸ Reduce the brush's **Opacity** to 35%, then paint another petal.

❹ Use the same brush to paint the same petal again.

STEP 9: Change the **Opacity** back to 100%, and change the **Mode** to **Multiply**.

STEP 10: Paint a different petal. ❺ Notice how different the color is, even though you're using the same foreground color. That's because the Multiply mode multiplies the base color (the image's original color) with the blending color (the **Foreground** color you've chosen for your brush). The resulting color is always darker (unless the base color is white, in which case the resulting color is unchanged). That's why this petal is now a darker color.

STEP 11: Now change the **Mode** to **Difference** and paint another petal. ❻ Surprise! The Difference mode looks at the information about the blend color and the base color, then subtracts one color from the other, depending on which has the greater brightness value. For most of us, that doesn't mean much, but it does mean Photoshop

Elements can do some cool things with color science to produce some exciting (and sometimes unexpected) results!

STEP 13: Change the **Mode** to **Dissolve**, set the **Opacity** to 50%, and paint another petal. The Dissolve mode works best with larger brushes so the speckles look more random.

STEP 13: Finally, set the **Mode** to **Darken** and change the Opacity back to 100% and paint one more petal.

Your final image should look something like this. ❼

Granted, this photo now looks like a bad cartoon. But the techniques you've just experimented with can be just the creative juice you need to repair, enhance, or even spice up a photograph, as you'll see in the next lesson.

❺ Change the **Opacity** to 100% and the **Mode** to **Multiply**.

❻ Change the **Mode** to **Difference** and paint another petal.

❼ Each petal uses a different combination of Mode and Opacity.

COLORIZING A BLACK-AND-WHITE PHOTO

If you've ever seen a hand-tinted black-and-white photo, you know how stunning the effect can be. Brushes are perfect for digitally colorizing portions of black-and-white photographs. Try it on one of your favorite photos. You can start with either a black and white or color photo.

STEP 1: Open a photograph.

STEP 2: Duplicate your original photo layer so you'll have a "clean" version to go back to if you need it.

STEP 3: If you're using a color photo, convert it to black and white. (If your photo is already black and white, skip to Step 4.) You can always convert a color image to grayscale by changing its mode (from the **Image** menu, point to **Mode**, then click

Grayscale). But a better way to remove color from an image is to desaturate it. This will retain the image's highlights and shadows and yield a richer image than converting the image to Grayscale mode. Here's how:

STEP 3A: From the **Layer** menu, point to **New Adjustment Layer**, then click **Hue/Saturation**. Check the box beside **Group With Previous Layer**, then click **OK**.

STEP 3B: In the dialog box that appears, drag the **Saturation** slider all the way to the left. This effectively desaturates your image of all color. ❶

STEP 3C: Merge the duplicate photo layer and the Hue/Saturation layer (press **SHIFT** and click the layers in the **Layers** palette, then open the **Layer** menu and click **Merge Layers**). The resulting merged layer is the layer you'll colorize.

STEP 4: Open the **Color Swatches** palette and load the **Foreground color** with the color of your choice.

❹

STEP 5: Select the **Brush** tool, open the **Brushes Preset** palette, and select the **Default Brushes** library. Then choose a soft round brush—the size depends on how much area you want to cover.

STEP 6: Change the brush's **Mode** to **Overlay**, and reduce the **Opacity** to 50%. If you want more saturated color, increase the opacity.

STEP 7: Paint over the areas of the photo you want to colorize. If you're painting a large area, start with a medium or large brush and paint as much of the area as you can. Then switch to a smaller brush and zoom in closely so that you can see clearly, then cover the edges. If you want a sharp edge, switch to a hard round brush for those areas. Experiment until you get the look you want.

⚙ TECH TIP

Where brush strokes overlap you may accidentally apply too much color. If this happens, use the **Eraser** tool with a soft brush and lowered opacity to gradually remove some of the color. Wouldn't it be great if it were this easy to remove real paint?

Here's a photo I colorized! ❷ ❸

Colorizing images is a surprisingly easy way to achieve eye-catching looks and put your own touch of personality into your photos.

Now that you understand the fundamentals of brushes, it's time to learn how to use them as rubber stamps.

❷ Before: My black-and-white photo.

❸ After: My colorized photo.

if you ask me what i came into the world to do,
i will tell you i came to

live out loud

using brushes as rubber stamps

In the first lesson of this chapter, you learned basic techniques for painting with brushes in Photoshop Elements. Now that you have the basics under your belt, it's time to move on to the really cool stuff.

The exercises in this lesson will show you how to use a brush like a rubber stamp—adding unique touches to your photos and your pages. You'll learn the difference between changing a brush's

blending mode and a layer's blending mode, you'll learn how to rotate and flip a layer, and you'll use a sketch filter called **Graphic Pen** to create a striking image.

First, however, you need to learn how to add new brush libraries to Photoshop Elements.

ADDING A NEW BRUSH LIBRARY
TO PHOTOSHOP ELEMENTS

Even though Photoshop Elements provides a large number of versatile brushes, there are many more that you can purchase or download from other sources.

You can even create your own brushes, which is exactly what you'll do in the next lesson. But first, let's talk about brush libraries.

Whenever you download brushes, they come as a set called a brush library. You can identify a Photoshop brush library by its *.abr* filename extension.

You can save the brush library anywhere on your computer's hard disk, but it's most convenient to place the library file in the *Brushes* folder in the Photoshop Elements program files. That way, the library name will appear in the **Brush Preset** palette the next time you start up Photoshop Elements.

To see how it's done, let's copy a new brush library from this book's CD to the Photoshop Elements *Brushes* folder on your computer's hard drive.

STEP 1: Close Photoshop Elements. New brush libraries won't appear in the **Brush Preset** palette until the program is restarted, so you might as well close it now.

STEP 2: First, locate the *Photoshop Elements* folder on your computer. Usually, you'll find it by opening the *Program Files* folder (*Applications* on a Mac), then the *Adobe* folder. Within the *Photoshop Elements* folder, open the *Presets* folder, then open the *Brushes* folder. This is the folder you will copy your new brushes into.

STEP 3: Now open the CD that came with this book, and locate the brush library called *dds2brushes.abr* (in the *other* folder). Copy it to the *Brushes* folder on your computer.

STEP 4: Restart Photoshop Elements and open the Editor workspace.

STEP 5: Check to make sure your new library is there by clicking the **Brush** tool, then opening the **Brush Preset** palette.

If you saved the dds2brushes library to the Photoshop Elements *Brushes* folder, the library should appear automatically in the list of libraries in the **Brushes** box. If you copied the library file into a different folder, you must first load the library before you can access its brushes. To do this, click the small arrow button on the right of the **Brush Preset** palette, and click **Load Brushes**. Then navigate to the folder where you copied the library file, select it, and click **Load**.

That's it! Now the brushes that came with this book are ready to use. You can load other brush libraries from online vendors, friends, or other sources in exactly the same way.

ⓘ INFO TIP

Photoshop Elements comes with a large number of default brushes you can use for a variety of effects. But that doesn't mean you can't have more! I've included a number of my own brushes on this book's CD for you. In addition, you can download brushes from a dizzying number of sources on the internet. Just search for "Photoshop Brushes" and you'll have more than enough places to get you started. Many online digital scrapbooking retailers also offer downloadable brushes just for scrapbookers. The things you'll learn in this lesson will also apply to any brushes you download later.

USING BRUSHES LIKE A STAMP

Although they're called brushes in Photoshop Elements because they simulate paint brushes, you'll be using them more like rubber stamps in this exercise. Just as you load a real stamp with ink and then apply it to your paper, you'll load your brush with the **Foreground** color and then click it once on your page instead of dragging it.

In the previous lesson, you painted directly onto an image. In this lesson, you'll place each stroke on a separate layer for maximum flexibility. That way, if you don't like it, you can simply delete the layer and do it again.

STEP 1: Open the *brushlayout.psd* file from the *other* folder on the CD. ❶

STEP 2: Select the *background* layer, then add a new layer and name it *brush 1*. (Selecting the background layer first ensures the new layer is between the *background* layer and the photo layers.)

STEP 3: Select the **Brush** tool and open the **Brush Preset** palette.

STEP 4: Click the **Brushes** box and select the **dds2brushes** library. ❷

STEP 5: Press **ENTER** to close the **Brush Preset** palette.

STEP 6: Make sure the *Lolly* color swatches are still loaded in the **Color Swatch** palette, then click **tangerine** to load it as the Foreground color.

STEP 7: Open the **Brush Preset** palette again, and click the **dds2floral** brush. ❸

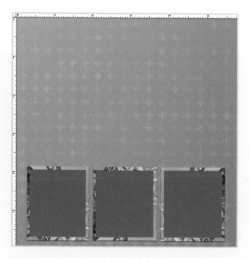

❶ Open the layout template, *brushlayout.psd*.

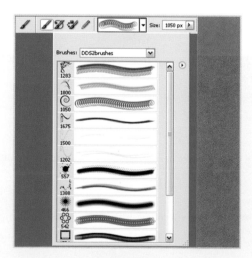

❷ Select the **dds2brushes** library.

STEP 8: In the options bar, set the brush **Size** to 1250 pixels, its **Mode** to **Normal**, and its **Opacity** to 40%.

STEP 9: Make sure the *brush 1* layer is selected, then click once inside your document to stamp the brush shape. **4**

STEP 10: Select the **Move** tool and position the stamped shape on the left edge of the document with a portion of it bleeding off the page. (In the **Move** tool's options bar, make sure the **Auto Select Layer** and **Show Bounding Box** options are unchecked.) You'll notice that part of the stamped image is hidden behind the photos layer. That's okay. This lets you see how it will look in your final layout as you position the stamped image on the page.

d DESIGN TIP

In this exercise, I like how it looks when the stamped image bleeds off the edge of the page, so the steps guide you to recreate this look. However, feel free to position the brushes wherever you like on your page.

STEP 11: Change the **Foreground** and **Background** colors back to the default black and white (click the small black and white icon in the toolbox, or type a lowercase D).

STEP 12: Now reverse the **Foreground** and **Background** colors so that the **Foreground** color is white. To do this, click the curved double-arrow icon beside the color boxes in the toolbox (or type a lowercase v).

STEP 13: Add a new layer and name it *brush 2*.

STEP 14: Select the **Brush** tool (the brush you used previously will still be active) and click once inside the document to stamp a white brush shape. **5**

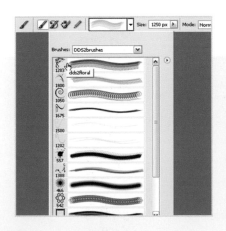

3 Select the **dds2floral** brush.

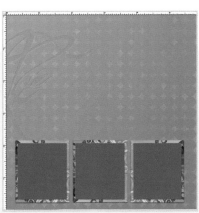

4 Click once inside your document to stamp the shape.

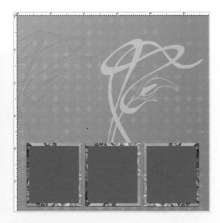

5 Click once to stamp a white shape on a new layer.

STEP 15: Select the **Move** tool and check the **Show Bounding Box** option in the options bar.

STEP 16: Use the bounding box handles to rotate the shape clockwise about 140% (the degree of rotation is shown in the options bar). Move it into the upper right corner, again with a portion bleeding off the page. ❻ Click **Commit** when you're finished.

STEP 17: Make sure *brush 2* is still selected. At the top of the **Layers** palette, click the **Blending Modes** box and select **Soft Light**. ❼ This mode simulates a diffused spotlight shining on the layer.

Because the brush was on its own layer and had no pixels to interact with, changing the brush's Mode to **Soft Light** wouldn't have generated a visible effect. But changing the layer's **Blending Mode** will because it will interact with the layers below it.

ⓣ **TECH TIP**

A layer's blending mode determines how its pixels blend with underlying pixels in the image. You can create a variety of special effects using blending modes.

STEP 18: Add a new layer, name it *brush 3* and select the **Brush** tool again. Change the **Size** to **600 pixels** and click once inside your page.

STEP 19: Flip this layer upside down. To do this, open the **Image** menu, point to **Rotate**, then click **Flip Layer Horizontal**. ❽ (Be careful to choose **Flip Layer Horizontal** and not **Flip Horizontal**, which will flip the entire layout.)

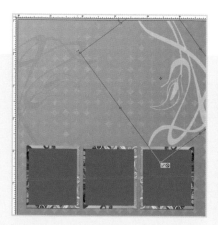

❻ Rotate the shape clockwise about 140%.

❼ Change the *brush 2* layer's blending mode to **Soft Light**.

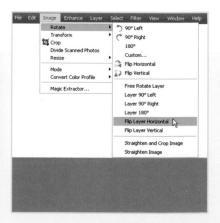

❽ Flip the layer horizontally.

STEP 20: Select the **Move** tool. Use the bounding box handles to rotate the shape slightly clockwise (about 33 degrees). Then click **Commit**.

STEP 21: Change this layer's blending mode to **Soft Light**, too. ❾

There! A beautiful background for your photos. But you know, I think we can take it just a little bit further. Let's try adding a special-effects photo to the background.

ADDING A PHOTO TO THE BACKGROUND

For this part of the exercise, you'll need a large digital photo to use as part of the background. The photo needs to be at least 1800 by 1800 pixels to fit the layout. (It doesn't matter if it's color or black and white.)

You'll also need three smaller photos to put into the layout at the end of the exercise. They can be black-and-white, color, sepia, or any style you like.

When you have your photos ready, you can continue with the following steps.

STEP 1: Select the background layer. That way, when you copy your photo into the document, it will be above the background, but below your stamped images.

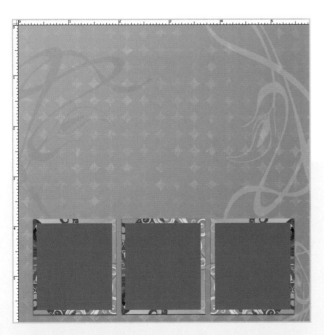

❾ Change the *brush 3* layer's blending mode to **Soft Light**.

STEP 2: Open the photo you want to use for the background.

Now you're going to change how this photo looks by applying a filter.

STEP 3: First, change the **Foreground** and **Background** colors back to the default black and white (click the small black and white icon in the toolbox, or type a lowercase D).

STEP 4: From the **Filter** menu, point to **Sketch**, then click **Graphic Pen**. When the **Filter Gallery** opens, use the zoom controls in the lower left corner to zoom out so you can see your photo in the preview area. ❶ Click **OK** to accept the default settings.

ⓘ TECH TIP

If your photo looks like a negative when you apply the **Graphic Pen** filter, check to make sure your **Foreground** color is black and the **Background** color is white. If these colors are reversed, the photo will appear to be a negative. You can use different colors in the boxes for different looks with the Graphic Pen filter, but for this exercise, you just need a black and white image.

STEP 5: Copy the changed photo into your document. The easiest way to do this is to click the **Move** tool, then drag the photo onto your layout. Use the bounding box corner handles to increase or reduce its size until it covers the page. (In Photoshop Elements 4.0 or earlier, remember to hold down the **SHIFT** key while you move the handles, so that the image doesn't distort.) ❷

❶ Apply the **Graphic Pen** filter to your photo.

❷ Copy a photo into your layout.

STEP 6: When you drag the photo into your document, it becomes a new layer. Change its name to *background photo*, just for clarity's sake.

STEP 7: Change the photo layer's **Blending Mode** to **Soft Light** and the **Opacity** to **40%**. (Depending on your photo, you may need to adjust the opacity up or down so it's visible but doesn't dominate your layout.) ❸

Next, you'll add your smaller photos.

PUTTING PHOTOS IN THE FRAMES

Now it's time to add three small photos to your layout. You could simply copy three photos into your layout, and then resize them and crop them until they fit inside the frame. But there's another way to do it that doesn't involve cropping—it's called a Clipping Group.

A Clipping Group is a group of layers to which you apply a mask. A mask is a shape you use to keep areas of a layer from being seen. With a Clipping Group, the bottommost mask layer (called the base layer) of the group defines the boundaries of all the layers of the group.

In this exercise, you'll copy in three photos, then use the photo masks to "clip" the photos so they fit behind the frame.

The nice thing about using a Clipping Group behind a frame is that you don't have to crop

❸ Change the photo layer's Blending Mode to Soft Light and Opacity to 40%.

any of your photo—the mask's shape will define the portion of the photo to be revealed, but those portions outside the boundaries of the mask won't be seen. You'll learn more about masks, including how to make your own, in Lesson 4 in this chapter.

It sounds far more complicated than it really is. Let's try it.

STEP 1: Open the first photo and drag it onto the layout document. It will probably be too large for the space allotted for it, so click the **Move** tool. Then drag the photo's corner handles to reduce its size until it is closer to the size of the gray photo area, but it doesn't have to be an exact fit. (In Photoshop Elements 4.0, remember to hold down the **SHIFT** key so the photo doesn't distort.) Then position the photo so it appears to be behind the first frame. The photo's outer edges will probably peek out from behind the frame—that's okay! ❶

STEP 2: In the **Layers** palette, rename your new photo layer to *photo 1*, and drag it up so that it's just above the *photo mask1* layer. ❷

STEP 3: Now you'll use the mask layer to "clip" the photo layer above it. With your new photo layer selected, open the **Layer** menu and click **Group with Previous**. ❸

See how the image now looks like it's been cropped to fit the space? It hasn't really been cropped—using a Clipping Group is a non-destructive way to hide the unwanted potions of photos! Take a look at the **Layers** palette. You can tell which layers are grouped: the photo 1 layer is indented, and it has a tiny arrow pointing to the base layer below it, indicating that the two layers are a Clipping Group. ❹

❶ Position the photo behind the first frame.

❷ Position the *photo 1* layer just above the *photo mask1* layer.

❸ Using a Clipping Group makes the photo the same shape as the mask.

STEP 4: Repeat Steps 1 - 3 for the other two photos. Remember to position each photo layer just above its mask layer, so that you can group the two of them together in a Clipping Group. ❺

STEP 5: Use the **Horizontal Type** tool to create a title and some journaling, if you like. ❻

Voila! Your gorgeous layout is finished. The brush stamps add a nice touch, don't they?

You've learned how to add a new brush library to your bag of tricks, how to use brushes like rubber stamps, and even how to add a cool photo effect to a background.

Now you're ready to create your own brushes and brush libraries.

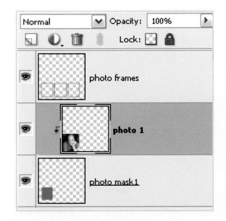

❹ The photo layer is in a Clipping Group with the mask layer, indicated by an indented thumbnail and a small arrow.

❺ Add two more photos to the layout.

❻ Here's my finished layout, with journaling and title added.

making your own brushes

By now, you've got the hang of Photoshop Elements' preset brush presets. You know how to customize them, enhance photos with them, and use them as stamps. Now it's time to move on to creating your own decorative brushes like the ones you may have seen digital scrapbooking experts use. Being able to design your own brushes gives you that extra element of creative control that can boost a really good layout to a really great layout.

In this lesson, you'll create several of your own brushes, and then you'll save them in their own brush library.

CREATING A NEW BRUSH

To get started, let's design a simple brush.

STEP 1: Create a new blank file named *firstbrushes*. Set the **Width** to 2400 pixels and the **Height** to 1800 pixels, the **Resolution** to 300 pixels, the **Color Mode** to RGB Color, and the **Background** to White. Don't turn on the grid for this exercise.

ⓣ TECH TIP
Brushes can't be bigger than 2500 pixels. Setting the width and height of your document in pixels ensures that your new brush will not exceed the 2500 pixel size limitation.

STEP 2: Click the **Brush** tool and reset the brush settings to their default settings (click the **Brush** tool icon on the left side of the options bar and click **Reset Tool**).

STEP 3: Click the **Create a new layer** button and name it *swoosh*.

STEP 4: From the **Brush Preset** palette, open the **Default Brushes** library, and select the **Hard Round 13 pixels** brush.

STEP 5: Reset the **Foreground** and **Background** colors to their default black and white by clicking the black and white boxes next to the color boxes in the toolbox, or by typing a lowercase D.

STEP 6: Using your mouse (or stylus or pen if you have a digitizing tablet), draw a large swoosh or swirl. ❶ By making your original artwork as large as possible (within the 2500 pixel limit), you ensure that your brushes will be nice and crisp at any size when you use them on your page layouts.

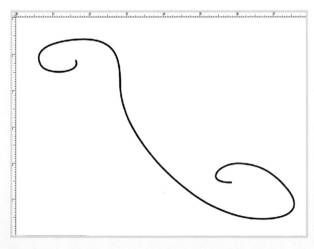
❶ Draw a swoosh or swirl.

ⓓ DESIGN TIP
Don't worry if your drawing is not as smooth as you'd like. Drawing with either a mouse or stylus takes practice—your strokes will improve with time. Start by drawing slowly, instead of swiftly like you would with a pencil, until you're comfortable drawing with a mouse or sylus. For now, just focus on drawing something that you can turn into a brush.

STEP 7: Now you'll define your drawing as a new brush. From the **Edit** menu, click **Define Brush**. Name your brush *myfirstbrush* and click **OK**.

2 The new brush is added to the bottom of the **Brush Preset** palette. Because you created a brush from a pre-drawn shape, it's considered a sampled brush. To Photoshop Elements, you've actually "sampled" the pixels in an image.

STEP 8: Turn off the visibility of the *swoosh* layer.

STEP 9: Create a new layer and name it *practice*.

STEP 10: In the **Brush Preset** palette, select your new brush and then click the **More Options** icon at the right side of the options bar. **3**

Now that you've created a new brush, you can make temporary changes to it just as you did to some of the preset brushes in previous lessons. Let's look at some of the options available in the **More Options** dialog box:

- **Spacing:** This option controls the distance between the brush marks as you drag the brush.
- **Hardness:** You used this option in this chapter's first lesson. But you can't change the hardness of sampled brushes, so this option is now unavailable.
- **Angle:** By typing a value in degrees or dragging the horizontal axis in the preview box, you can specify the angle by which your brush is rotated.
- **Roundness:** You can enter a new value or drag either of the two black circles in the preview box to make your brush more elliptical and less round.
- The other options (**Fade, Hue Jitter,** and **Scatter**) give you more control over your brush when you are using it like a paint brush in more traditional painting techniques. If you intend to use Photoshop Elements as a painting program, you can read more about these options in Photoshop Elements' Help. But for our purposes, leave these options at their default settings.

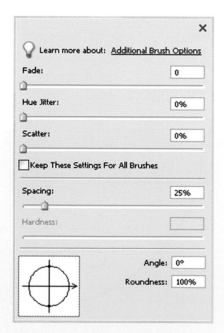

3 Select your new brush, then click the **More Options** icon in the options bar.

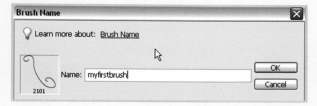

2 Name your new brush *myfirstbrush*.

Tablet Users: If you are using a digitizing tablet, like those from Wacom, you can set the sensitivity of a brush so it reacts to the amount of pressure you apply with the stylus or pen. To make the tool tip size change with pressure, select **Tablet Options** in the options bar. Then choose **Size**.

You can set pen pressure for other brush characteristics, too. The **Tablet Options** dialog box contains settings that vary the **Opacity, Scatter, Roundness,** and **Hue Jitter** according to pen pressure. For more information on these settings, see Adobe Photoshop Elements Help.

STEP 11: When you're finished looking at the available options, press **ENTER** to close the **More Options** dialog box.

STEP 12: Now you're ready to try out your new brush. In the options bar, change the **Size** to something smaller, like 900 pixels, then click once inside your document. (Tablet users: Don't forget to try the pressure settings.)

STEP 13: Click the **More Options** icon again and set the **Angle** to 90 degrees. Click once again inside your document. ❹

STEP 14: Experiment with other settings and adjustments, clicking in your document after each change to see its affect.

When you're finished experimenting with your new brush, you can move on to the next exercise.

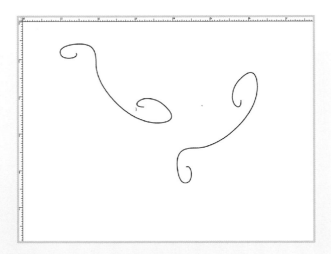

❹ Change your brush's settings and try out each change.

CREATING ADDITIONAL BRUSHES

Now that you've created your first brush, let's add more custom brushes to create a library. You already know how to draw a swirl or a swoosh. How would you like to turn your swoosh into a dotted line? It's very easy to do.

STEP 1: Turn off the visibility of all layers except the white background.

STEP 2: Create a new layer and name it *dotted*.

STEP 3: From the **Brush Preset** palette, select the **Hard Round 19 pixels** brush and change its **Size** to 30 pixels.

STEP 4: Click the **More Options** icon and adjust the **Spacing** slider to 200%. As you move the slider, watch the preview box of the **Brush Preset** palette and notice how the smooth brush stroke changes to dots. ❶ Press **ENTER** to close the **More Options** dialog box.

STEP 5: Now draw another swoosh. ❷ This time, your drawing has dots instead of a smooth stroke. If you want smaller dots, select a smaller round brush and repeat Step 4.

STEP 6: From the **Edit** menu, click **Define Brush**, give your second brush a new name, and click **OK**.

STEP 7: Create a new layer and name it *practice dotted*.

STEP 8: Turn off the visibility of all layers except the *practice dotted* and *background layers*.

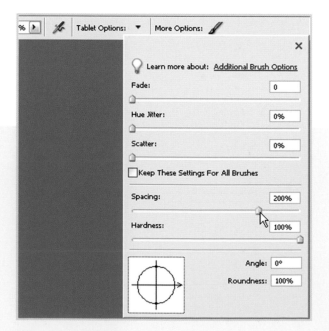

❶ Change the **Spacing** to 200% and the brush stroke will change to dots.

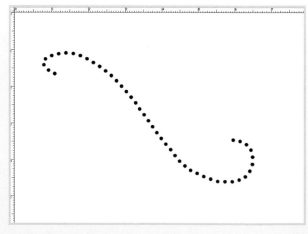

❷ Draw another swoosh.

STEP 9: Now try out your second brush. First, click it once to see what it looks like. Then change the **Size** of your brush to something smaller, such as 500 pixels. Click inside your document to see what that one looks like. Feel free to test additional sizes and rotations.

When you're finished experimenting, you'll be ready to create your own brush library.

CREATING A BRUSH LIBRARY

Now that you've defined two new brushes, you're ready to create your own brush library. The easiest way to do this is to use the **Preset Manager**. This tool lets you manage the presets of different types of libraries. In Chapter 1, you used the **Preset Manager** to manage the patterns you made. In this exercise, you'll use the **Preset Manager** to manage your brush libraries.

STEP 1: Open the **Preset Manager** from the **Edit** menu. For **Preset Type**, select **Brushes**. You'll

see all the default preset brushes, plus the two you created. (Scroll to the bottom of the list to see your added brushes.) **❶**

STEP 2: Select the two new brushes you created. (Press **SHIFT** and click to select multiple brushes.)

STEP 3: Click **Save Set**. Name your set *My First Brushes*, then specify a location for the library set, and click **Done**. **❷** I strongly recommend you save the library in the Photoshop Elements *Brushes* folder so it will appear in the **Brush Preset** palette every time you start the program.

STEP 4: Load the brush library so you can access the brushes from the **Brush Preset** palette. To do this, you can either quit Photoshop Elements and restart it, or you can open the **Brush Preset** palette and click the small arrow button to the right of the palette. Select **Load Brushes**, navigate to the brush library you just saved, and click **Load**.

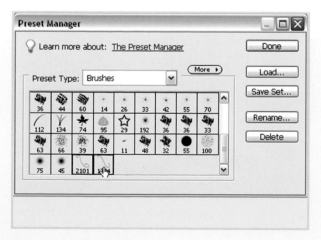

❶ Open the **Preset Manager**.

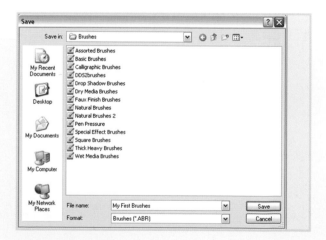

❷ Save your brush library.

The **Brush Preset** palette now shows only your two new brushes, which for now are the only brushes in your library. ❸

If you saved the library to a different folder than the default *Brushes* folder, Photoshop Elements won't automatically load it when you restart the program. You will have to repeat this step to load the library yourself every time you restart Photoshop Elements.

STEP 5: Close the *firstbrushes* document. Since this is only a practice document, you don't need to save it.

Now that you know how to use Photoshop Elements' standard brush presets to create you own swirl brushes, you can explore some other sources for creative brushes.

CREATING A PHOTO-BASED BRUSH

Believe it or not, photos of your kids, pets, or even yourself make excellent brushes. For this exercise, a close-up of a person's face will work best. Here's how to convert it into a brush.

STEP 1: Open a favorite high-resolution photo and save it with a new name so that you won't risk altering your original.

STEP 2: Define this image as a brush just as you did in the previous lesson: from the **Edit** menu, click **Define Brush**. Then give this new brush a name and click **OK**. Your photo brush now appears in the **Brush Preset** palette along with the two you created earlier. ❶

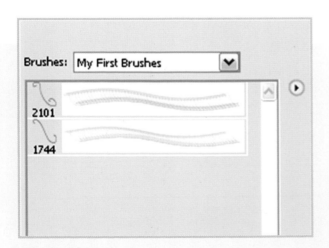

❸ The **Brush Preset** palette now shows only your two new brushes.

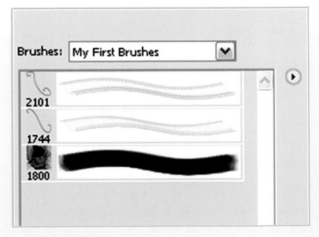

❶ The **Brush Preset** palette now shows three new brushes.

If the **Define Brush** option is grayed out and unavailable, your image may be too large. It must be no larger than 2500 pixels in either width or height. To check the size of your photo, open the Image menu, point to **Resize**, and click **Image Size**. Look at the **Pixel Dimensions**—neither the width nor height can be more than 2500 pixels. If it's too large, you can resize your photo. To do that, check the **Resample Image** checkbox at the bottom of the dialog box. Make sure **Constrain Proportions** is checked. Then, in the **Pixel Dimensions** box, change the larger of the dimensions to a number below 2500. (The other dimension will change automatically.) Click **OK**. Now you should be able to define the photo as a brush.

STEP 3: Now you'll make another brush from this photo, but first you'll apply a filter to modify it. To do this, first duplicate the photo's layer (click **More** in the **Layers** palette and select **Duplicate Layer**).

STEP 4: Make sure the **Foreground** color is black and the **Background** color is white.

STEP 5: From the **Filter** menu, point to **Sketch**, then click **Photocopy**. The **Filter Gallery** opens and your image appears in the preview window. Use the zoom controls in the lower left corner to zoom out so you can see more of your photo. ❷ Use the sliders to make any adjustments you wish to the **Detail** and **Darkness** settings, then click **OK**. ❸

ⓓ DESIGN TIP

The Photocopy filter is great for converting photos to line art, too.

STEP 6: Now turn this image into a brush, too. (From the **Edit** menu, click **Define Brush**, give it a name, and click **OK**.)

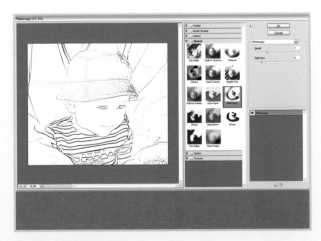

❷ Apply the **Photocopy** filter.

❸ The Photocopy filter has been applied to the photograph.

STEP 7: Now add one more brush based on your photo. First, duplicate the original photo's layer again and move the duplicate to the top of the **Layers** palette.

STEP 8: From the **Filter** menu, point to **Sketch**, then click **Graphic Pen**. Set the **Stroke Length** to 10, the **Light/Dark Balance** to 50, and the **Stroke Direction** to **Right Diagonal**. Then click **OK**.

STEP 9: Define this image as a brush (see Step 6).

STEP 10: Now that you have five brushes in your library, it's a good idea to save the library again. From the **Brush Preset** palette, click the small

arrow button and select **Save Brushes**. Navigate to the library you created earlier and select it. Then click **Save** and replace your library. Each time you add a brush in the future, remember to save your library.

STEP 11: Close your photo document. We're finished with this photo. But we're not finished making brushes!

STEP 12: Quit Photoshop Elements and restart it. That will make your new brush library appear in the **Brush Preset** palette when you create a new document in the next exercise.

CREATING A DOTTED CIRCULAR BRUSH

When I teach digital scrapbooking classes, one of the most popular requests is to create dotted circular brushes. This exercise will show you how to create a brush that "stamps" a circle of dots on your layouts.

STEP 1: Create a new document named *circledots*. Set both the **Width** and **Height** to 8", the **Resolution** to 300, the **Color Mode** to Grayscale, and the **Background** to Transparent.

STEP 2: From the **View** menu, turn on the **Ruler** and **Grid**.

STEP 3: Select the **Brush** tool, open the **Brush Preset** palette, then select **Default Brushes** in the **Brushes** box.

STEP 4: Select the **Hard Round 19 pixels** brush, and change its **Size** to 40 pixels.

STEP 5: Click the **More Options** icon and change the **Spacing** to 200%, the **Angle** to 90 degrees, and the **Roundness** to 30%. (**Leave Fade, Hue Jitter, and Scatter** at 0%, and leave **Hardness** at 100%).

STEP 6: Position your cursor on the far left side of your document window at the vertical center point (4" on the vertical ruler). Press and hold **SHIFT** while you click there and then click again directly across on the far right side of your document window. ❶

STEP 7: From the **Filter** menu, choose **Distort**, then click **Polar Coordinates**. ❷ Make sure **Rectangular to Polar** is selected, then click **OK**. Now you have a dotted circle you can define as a brush.

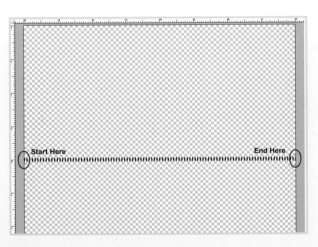

❶ Draw a straight line across the center of the page.

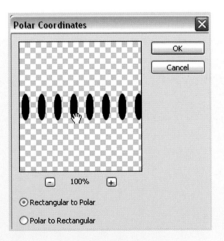

❷ Apply the **Polar Coordinates** filter.

ⓓ DESIGN TIP

Because your circle is large (over 1200 pixels), you can create pages using the brush at very small sizes or very large sizes without any distortion or loss of quality. Remember, all you have to do to change the brush size is to change its **Size** in the options bar.

STEP 8: From the **View** menu, turn off the **Grid**.

STEP 9: Open the **Brush Preset** palette and select or load your brushes library that you saved earlier.

STEP 10: Now open the **Edit** menu and click **Define Brush** to turn this circle of dots into a brush.

STEP 11: Save your brush library again so that your new brush will appear in it next time you restart Photoshop Elements. (From the **Brush Preset** palette, click the small arrow button and select **Save Brushes** from the bottom of the menu.)

STEP 12: Have fun! Continue creating and adding brushes to your library.

You're not limited to just one brush library. You can create as many brush libraries as you like, depending on how you want to organize your brushes. Just remember to save the libraries as you add new brushes to them, so you don't lose all the hard work you put in.

The final lesson in this chapter gets even more creative! You'll learn more ways to use brushes creatively, as well as additional tips and techniques for creating even more special effects with Photoshop Elements.

more tips and tricks

As we near the end of these lessons, I find there are still so many things I want to share with you. I suppose those will have to wait for the "sequel to the sequel"! To close out this chapter, though, I've included a few of my favorite "must-have" techniques for adding interest to your digital scrapbook pages.

In this lesson, you'll learn how to give your backgrounds and embellishments that "grunge" or distressed look, using brushes and the **Eraser** tool. Then you'll explore some beautifully creative—but deceptively simple—edge effects for your images.

MAKING GRUNGE BRUSHES

Sometimes nothing will do like a nice, distressed look that I call "grunge." In Chapter 1, you added a semi-transparent "distressed" layer to a background to give it the grunge look. To add that layer, you copied the *distressed.png* overlay file from the CD.

In this exercise, you'll learn how to create and maintain a set of grunge brushes for your own distressed look. You'll find that using these brushes is one of the fastest ways to add quick and dirty distress to your backgrounds and photos.

ⓓ DESIGN TIP

I love shooting distressed backgrounds. I'm constantly scouring the city for abandoned warehouses and industrial construction sites where I shoot close-ups of the many interesting textures. But one of my favorite sources is my neighborhood coffee shop.

ⓘ INFO TIP

When shooting distressed backgrounds, get as close as your camera will allow and use the highest possible resolution. The resulting image will give you the most flexibility to work with.

The brick walls and concrete floors are rich with complex textures. Look around your neighborhood. What textures can you capture for your own unique looks?

Let's open a photo of my favorite coffee shop's concrete floor, and turn it into a grunge brush.

STEP 1: Open the file *dds2grungephoto.jpg* from the *other* folder on the CD. ❶

STEP 2: Set the foreground color to white and the background color to black.

STEP 3: Duplicate the photo layer. You'll be modifying the duplicate layer, so you can go back to the original layer if you need to.

❶ Open the file *dds2grungephoto.jpg*.

STEP 4: First, apply the **Graphic Pen** filter to the photo. To do this, open the **Filter** menu, point to **Sketch**, then click **Graphic Pen**. ❷

STEP 5: In the **Filter Gallery**, use the zoom controls to zoom out until you can see your image. Change the **Stroke Length** to 3, the **Light/Dark Balance** to 50 and the **Stroke Direction** to Horizontal. Then click **OK**.

STEP 6: Select the **Brush** tool and open the **Brush Preset** palette.

STEP 7: Open the **dds2brushes** library. This is where you will store the new brush you're creating.

STEP 8: From the **Edit** menu, click **Define Brush**. Name your new brush *grungebrush1*.

STEP 9: Remember, you have to save the library now, or your new brush won't appear the next time you use Photoshop Elements. From the **Brush Preset** palette, click the small arrow button and select **Save Brushes**. Select the **dds2brushes** library, then click **Save** and replace the library.

STEP 10: Close the *dds2grungephoto.jpg* file.

Your new brush is ready to use!

❷ Apply the **Graphic Pen** filter to the photo.

CREATING A NEW GRUNGE BACKGROUND

Now you can use your new grunge brush to create a background page. Guess what? You can use custom brushes as eraser tips, too, with the **Eraser** tool. It's just like stamping, but instead of applying "ink" to a layer, it removes it. Here's how.

STEP 1: Create a new blank file named *brushbackground*. Set both the **Width** and **Height** to 6", the **Resolution** to 300 pixels, the **Color Mode** to RGB Color, and the **Background** to Transparent. You don't need to turn on the grid for this exercise.

STEP 2: Now you're going to add two new colors to the **Color Swatches** palette and use them as the foreground and background colors. First, you have to open the **Color Picker**. To do this, click the **Foreground** color box in the toolbox.

STEP 3: In the **Color Picker**, you can click an area of the large color spectrum to choose a color, or you can specify a color by typing in values for the Red, Green and Blue (RGB) settings. In this case, you want to specify a particular color, so set **R** to 118, **G** to 132, and **B** to 22. Then click **OK**. ❶

STEP 4: Now that this new color is the **Foreground** color, you can add it to the **Color Swatches** palette. Open the **Color Swatches** palette, and position the cursor over an empty space in the bottom row of the **Color Swatches** palette. (The cursor turns into the **Paint Bucket** tool.) ❷ Then click to add the new color. Name it *avocado* and click **OK**.

STEP 5: Now switch this color to the Background color by clicking the small, curved double-headed arrow next to the color boxes.

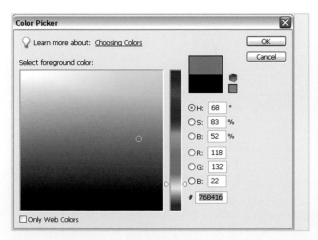

❶ Specify the **RGB** values to select a particular color.

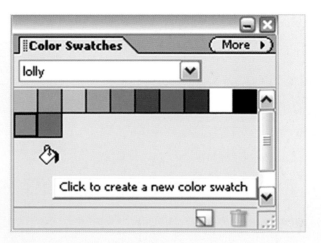

❷ To add a color to the **Color Swatches** palette, click an empty space in the palette.

STEP 6: Repeat Steps 2 - 4 to define a new **Foreground** color and add it to the **Color Swatches** palette. For this color, set **R** to 221, **G** to 157, and **B** to 119. Name it *salmon*.

Now you should have the **Foreground** color set to **salmon** and the **Background** color set to **avocado**. (If not, click the double-headed arrow next to the color boxes to switch the colors.)

ⓣ TECH TIP
You can only add a color to the **Color Swatches** palette when it is loaded as the **Foreground** color.

STEP 7: Fill the *Background* layer of your document with the **Foreground** color (salmon). (From the **Edit** menu, click **Fill Layer**, and for **Use** select **Foreground Color**.) ❸

STEP 8: Create a new layer and name it *color*.

STEP 9: Fill the new layer with the **Background** color (avocado).

STEP 10: Select the **Eraser** tool  from the toolbox. It's time to grunge up your background!

STEP 11: Open the **Brush Preset** palette, select the **dds2brushes** library, and select the **grungebrush1 brush** you created earlier.

STEP 12: Change the brush **Size** to 2500 pixels (the maximum size allowed), so that it will cover the entire page. Set the **Mode** to **Brush** and the **Opacity** to 100%. ❹

❸ Fill the *Background* layer with **salmon**

❺ Click the **Eraser** tool once to create a grunge background.

❹ Set the brush **Size** to 2500 pixels, **Mode** to **Brush**, and **Opacity** to **100%.**

STEP 13: Select the *color* layer, then position the Eraser tool over the page and click once. **⑤** Voila! Instant grunge background.

Making grunge backgrounds is just that easy. The Eraser tool is a powerful feature, and you can use it with any brush in your libraries!

ⓓ DESIGN TIP

If you want to make a background that's larger than 2500 pixels, just stamp the eraser as many times as you need to cover the area. You can undo steps and repeat them if necessary until you get just the right look. Or, use the Eraser tool with a soft round brush tip to selectively remove portions of the background.

ⓣ TECH TIP

The Eraser technique works great for distressing type fonts, too. Try creating your own set of grunge alphabets.

ADDING CREATIVE EDGE EFFECTS

I can't finish this chapter without showing you a few of my favorite—and easy—techniques for |adding appealing edge effects to your photos. First, you'll see how quick and simple it is to add a soft edge around your image. Then you'll explore the variety of crop shapes that Photoshop Elements provides.

In this exercise, you'll use one of your own photos to experiment with different edge effects.

CREATING A SOFT EDGE

STEP 1: Open one of your own color photos, and save it with a new name so that you won't risk altering your original. ❶

STEP 2: From the **View** menu, turn on the **Ruler** and **Grid**.

STEP 3: Change the **Foreground** and **Background** colors to the defaults (black and white).

STEP 4: Duplicate the photo layer, name the duplicate *soft edge*, and then select the duplicate layer.

STEP 5: Turn off the visibility of the original photo layer.

STEP 6: Select the **Rectangular Marquee** tool and draw a selection marquee about ¼" inside your photo. ❷ Use the ruler and grid to help you draw.

STEP 7: From the **Select** menu, choose **Feather**. Set the **Feather Radius** to **15 pixels**, and click **OK**. ❸ Notice that the corners of the selection marquee are now rounded. ❹ This means your selection is feathered. (It doesn't mean the selection marquee is really changed to a rounded rectangle—you have to use the **Rounded Rectangle Shape** tool for that.) The higher you set the radius, the softer the edge will be.

STEP 8: Because you want to delete the outer edge of the photo, you have to invert the selection marquee, so open the **Select** menu and click **Inverse**. Then press **DEL** to remove the edge, and press **ESC** to turn off the marquee. ❺

There you have your soft-edge photo. Wasn't that easy?

❶ Open a favorite photo and save a copy of it with a new name.

❷ Use the **Rectangular Marquee** tool to draw a selection marquee ¼" inside your photo.

❸ Set the **Feather Radius** to **15 pixels**.

❹ The selection marquee's corners become rounded, indicating the selection is feathered.

❺ Delete the outer edge of the photo.

DRAWING A FREEHAND EDGE

Now try drawing a freehand edge.

STEP 1: Duplicate the original photo layer again and name the new layer *freehand*. Drag it to the top of the **Layers** palette.

STEP 2: Turn off the visibility of all layers except your new *freehand* layer.

STEP 3: Turn off the grid. You won't need it for this exercise.

STEP 4: Select the **Lasso** tool. This tool lets you draw a selection marquee by hand, instead of using the very straight edges of the **Rectangular Marquee** tool. (In the **Lasso** tool's options bar, make sure the regular **Lasso** tool is selected, and not the **Magnetic Lasso** tool.)

STEP 5: Draw a selection marquee surrounding your photo about ¼" inside the margins. Don't try to be too neat—allow the line to be jagged and free-flowing. ❶

STEP 6: From the **Select** menu, click **Inverse**, then delete the outer edge. ❷

STEP 7: Before you remove the selection marquee, decide whether you want to leave the edge hard or soften it. If you'd like to soften it, you can feather it like you did earlier. (From the **Select** menu, click **Feather** and set the **Feather Radius** to **15 pixels**.)

STEP 8: Now press **DEL** again and press **ESC** to turn off the marquee.

Your photo now has a soft, wandering edge.

❶ Use the **Lasso** tool to draw a marquee around the photo.　　❷ Invert the selection, then delete the outer edge.

USING MASKS TO CREATE EDGES

You can make more edges by using Photoshop Elements' Crop Shapes to create masks. To use a mask, you place the mask over a photo, select the area outside the mask, then delete that area. Let's try a Crop Shape to create a distressed edge.

STEP 1: Duplicate the original photo layer again and name the new layer *photoshape1*. Drag it to the top of the **Layers** palette.

STEP 2: Turn off the visibility of all layers except your new *photoshape1* layer.

STEP 3: Select the **Custom Shape** tool.

STEP 4: In the options bar, click the **Shape** box to open the **Custom Shape Picker**. Then click the small arrow button on the **Custom Shape Picker**, and click **Crop Shapes**. ❶ The **Custom Shape Picker** now shows various **Crop Shapes**.

STEP 5: From the **Custom Shape Picker**, click **Crop Shape 8**.

STEP 6: Starting about ⅛" inside the upper left corner of your photo, click and drag to draw the Crop Shape mask. ❷

STEP 7: Select the mask's shape by pressing **CTRL** (**CMD** on a **Mac**) and clicking the *Shape 1* layer's thumbnail in the **Layers** palette. ❸

STEP 8: Turn off the visibility of the *Shape 1* layer.

STEP 9: Select the *photoshape1* layer.

STEP 10: Invert the selection marquee.

STEP 11: Before you delete the selection, decide if you want a jagged edge or a softer edge. If you want the edge to stay jagged, skip to Step 12. If you want to soften the edge, choose **Feather** from the **Select** menu. The example has a **Feather Radius** of 5 pixels.

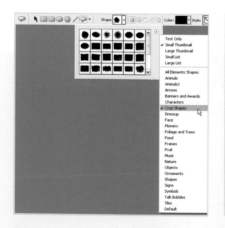

❶ From the **Custom Shape Picker**, select **Crop Shapes**.

❷ Draw the Crop Shape mask about ⅛" inside your photo's margins.

❸ Select the mask's shape.

STEP 12: Delete the ouler edge. ⑤

STEP 13: Turn off the selection marquee and admire your new edge.

Using a Crop Shape as a mask is nice and easy. Feel free to experiment with other Crop Shapes!

CREATING YOUR OWN CROP SHAPE

Can't find the Crop Shape you want? Make your own!

STEP 1: Duplicate the original photo layer again and name the new layer *photoshape2*. Drag it to the top of the **Layers** palette.

STEP 2: Turn off the visibility of all layers except your new *photoshape2* layer.

STEP 3: Create a new layer and name it *mask shape 2*.

STEP 4: Fill the new *mask shape 2* layer with black.

STEP 5: Select the **Eraser** tool, and choose an interesting brush. (The example uses the **dds2bigsplotch** brush, with its **Size** set to 75 pixels.) Then erase freehand along the edges of the photo until you have a look you like. You can use any brush you like—try several to see what they look like. ❶ Now you have your mask.

❹ Don't use feathering if you want a hard edge.

❸ Use feathering to create a softer edge.

❶ Use the **Eraser** tool to erase the outer edge.

STEP 6: Select the mask's shape by pressing **CTRL** (**CMD** on a **Mac**) and clicking the *mask shape 2* layer's thumbnail in the **Layers** palette.

STEP 7: Turn off the visibility of the *mask shape 2* layer.

STEP 8: Select the *photoshape2 layer*.

STEP 9: Invert the selection marquee.

STEP 10: Delete the outer edge. ❷

STEP 11: Turn off the selection marquee. There you have it—your own custom edge!

STEP 12: If you like the new mask you created, save it as a PNG file to use later. When you're ready to use it again, just open and copy it into your layout. Then repeat Steps 8 through 10.

Let's try one more masking exercise, shall we?

CREATING A MASK FOR A CLIPPING GROUP

Earlier in this chapter, you used a Clipping Group to conceal a portion of a photo behind a frame. In this exercise, you'll go a little further and create your own Clipping Group mask.

STEP 1: Duplicate the original *background* layer.

STEP 2: Turn off the visibility of all layers except your new *background copy* layer.

STEP 3: Create a new layer and name it *frame*. It should be positioned just above the *background copy* layer.

STEP 4: With the *frame* layer selected, use any brush you like to draw a decorative frame around the photo. ❶ In the example, I used the **dds2swirly1** brush in two different colors.

❷ Delete the outer edge.

STEP 5: Create a new layer and name it *mask*.

STEP 6: In the **Layers** palette, drag the *mask* layer down so it's between the *background copy* layer and the *frame* layer. Remember, your mask layer must be below the photo you want to mask.

STEP 7: Make sure the **Foreground** and **Background** colors are set to the default black and white (click the small black and white icon in the toolbox, or type a lowercase D).

STEP 8: Make sure the *mask* layer is selected, then use the **Rectangular Marquee** tool to draw the shape of the "mask" in the size you want.

STEP 9: With the selection marquee still active, fill the selection with black. ❷ It will cover up the photo, but don't worry. When you're done, the portion of the photo under the rectangular mask will show, and the portion outside it will be hidden.

STEP 10: Turn off the selection marquee by pressing **ESC**.

STEP 11: In the **Layers** palette, drag the photo layer (*background copy*) so that it's just above the mask layer and just below the frame layer. ❸ The order of the layers is important, so make sure your layers are now in this order:

- *frame*
- *background copy (photo)*
- *mask*

Now you'll use the Clipping Group feature to hide the portions of the photo that are outside the boundaries of your mask.

❶ Use brushes to draw a frame around the photo.

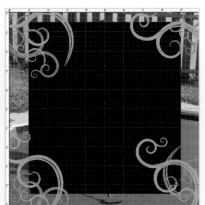

❷ Use the tool to draw a mask.

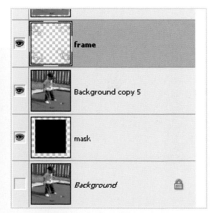

❸ Your layers should be in this order.

STEP 12: Select the *photo* layer, then open the **Layer** menu and click **Group with Previous**. Your photo has now been "clipped" to match the shape of the mask you created. ❹ ❺ The outer edges of the photo haven't been deleted—they're still intact. They're just hidden by the mask. (To remove a Clipping Group, just select the *photo* layer again, open the **Layer** menu, and choose **Ungroup**.)

Now your photo and frame are ready to be copied into a layout of your choice.

❹ Use a Clipping Group to clip the photo to match the mask's shape.

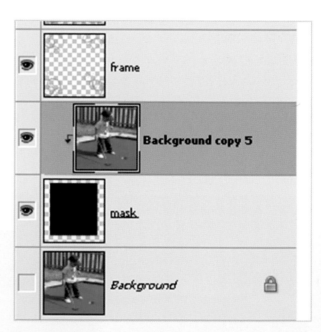

❺ The photo layer is grouped with the mask layer in a Clipping Group.

MORE TIPS FOR CLIPPING GROUPS

Clipping Groups are easy to make, and so useful. To make a frame template you can use over and over with different photos, just create a PSD file with a mask layer and a frame layer. Then, when you're ready to frame a photo, just copy the photo into the file, make sure the photo layer is between the mask and frame layers, and create a Clipping Group. It's that simple!

You can create an entire layout with several framed photos on it just as easily as one. Remember in Lesson 2 of this chapter, when you added three photos to the small frames on a layout from the CD? You can make your own layout with multiple frames, too. Just create a mask layer for each photo and save the whole layout as a layered PSD file. Then, when you're ready to use it, just add your photos and use the Clipping Group feature to group the photos with their respective masks.

Try using shapes other than rectangles for your mask layer in a Clipping Group. You can even use an alphabet shape as a mask! Use your imagination and create any shape you want as a mask.

You can even add more layers to a Clipping Group, so that multiple layers are clipped to the same mask shape. To add a new layer to a Clipping Group, position the layer directly above the layer that's already grouped, then from the **Layer** menu, click **Group with Previous** again. Remember, the mask must always be the base layer of a Clipping Group.

MORE FRAMING TIPS

Now you know how to create edge effects by using the **Eraser** tool, using Crop Shapes as masks, using masks you create from scratch, and using a Clipping Group. But there are other options, too!

Photoshop Elements has additional photo framing effects in the **Artwork and Effects** palette (**Styles and Effects** palette in Photoshop Elements 4.0). For more information on these frames, see Photoshop Elements Help. They're simple to use and well documented.

In addition, there are plenty of free brushes and photo frames on the internet. Just search for "Photoshop brushes" or "Photoshop frames." Be prepared to spend hours browsing, though!

Now it's time to exercise your creativity. Use your own brushes, the ones from the CD, and new edges you've learned to create to build a page layout. The gallery has examples of great layouts using the techniques you've learned in this book and the elements on the CD. Remember, you're only limited by your imagination. And that's what makes digital scrapbooking so cool!

CONGRATULATIONS!

You graduate! You've finished all the lessons in this book with flying colors, and you're probably itching to put what you've learned to work. Go for it!

Use what you've learned about creating backgrounds, digital embellishments, frames, and special effects to start creating your own fabulous layouts.

The next chapter is a handy, quick reference of the major tasks you learned in this book. Can't remember how to define a pattern? Forgot how to make a drop shadow? The basic steps are outlined for you again, so you can review them in a flash.

The final chapter of this book is a gallery of examples created by some of the brightest designers around, using the techniques in this book. I think you'll enjoy seeing them.

d DESIGN TIP

Don't forget to explore the CD that came with this book—I've designed plenty of backgrounds, elements, templates and more to spark your creativity as you create your own unique, beautiful, and personal scrapbook layouts. But remember, my elements are just a start. Now that you know how to create your own digital designs for scrapbooking, the sky's the limit!

remind me!

Now that you've finished all of the exercises, I hope you'll jump right into creating interesting digital scrapbook pages using your new skills. That means you may need to refer back to this book from time to time until you're comfortable with the new techniques you've learned. That's why I named this chapter Remind Me!

In the middle of creating an element and need a quick refresher? Turn here! Can't remember how to define a pattern or a new brush? Check here! All the major tasks you learned in this book's exercises are summarized here, with just the few key steps you need to get you going.

Remember, too, that Photoshop Elements Help is another great resource. Don't hesitate to use it.

CHANGE THE FOREGROUND AND BACKGROUND COLORS

To change the **Foreground** or **Background** color:

1. Click the **Foreground** or **Background** color box in the toolbox.

2. In the **Color Picker,** click a color in the spectrum or specify a color's RGB settings.

3. Click **OK**.

USE THE COLOR SWATCHES PALETTE

To add a set of swatches to the **Color Swatches** palette:

1. Open **Window > Color Swatches**.

2. In the palette, click **More > Load Swatches** to add to the existing set or **More > Replace Swatches** to replace the existing set.

3. Navigate to the swatch library. Click **Load**.

To add a color to the palette:

1. Set the **Foreground** color in the toolbox to the color you want to add.

2. Click an empty space in the palette's bottom row.

3. Name the color and click **OK**.

CREATE AND USE PATTERNS

To create and define a pattern:

1. Use the **Custom Shape** tool to draw your pattern.

2. Use the **Rectangular Marquee** tool to select the pattern.

3. If it's not a part of your pattern, turn off the *Background* layer's visibility.

4. Select the *Background* layer.

5. Open **Edit > Define Pattern**, name the pattern, and click **OK**.

To save your patterns as a set with the **Preset Manager**:

1. Open **Edit > Preset Manager**.

2. In the **Preset Type** box, select **Patterns**.

3. Press **SHIFT** or **CTRL** (**CMD** on a Mac) **+ click** to select your patterns.

4. Click **Save Set**, name your set, and click **Save**.

To fill a selection with a pattern:

1. Use a **Marquee** tool or press **CTRL** (**CMD** on a Mac) **+ click** a layer's thumbnail to select a portion of a layer.

2. Select the *Background* layer.

3. Open **Edit > Fill Selection > Use: Pattern**. Choose a pattern in the **Pattern picker** and click **OK**.

4. If your pattern isn't listed, click the arrow in the **Pattern picker**, then select **Load > Patterns** (or **Replace > Patterns**), navigate to your patterns, then click **Load**.

To make patterned background "paper":

1. Open a new document in your page size.

2. Fill the background with a solid color.

3. Open **Edit > Fill Layer > Use: Pattern**.

4. Select your pattern and click **OK**.

5. Save your "paper" as a JPEG file.

CUSTOMIZE AN ELEMENT'S TEMPLATE

To change the color of one of the templates on the CD:

1. Open the element's template file from the CD.

2. Select the element's layer.

3. Make sure the layer's transparent pixels are locked.

4. Open **Window > Color Swatches** and select a color, or click the **Foreground** color swatch and select a color using the **Color Picker**.

5. Open **Edit > Fill Layer > Use: Foreground Color** and click **OK**.

6. If the element is multi-layered, repeat Steps 2 – 5 for each layer.

To copy a pattern onto an element's template:

1. Open a background file.

2. Open **Image > Resize > Image Size**.

3. Check **Resample Image**, then set the width and height to the approximate size of the template. Click **OK**.

4. Open **Select > All**.

5. Copy the selection, click inside the element's document, then paste the selection. Close the background file.

6. Select the pasted layer, then press **CTRL** (**CMD** on a Mac) **+ click** inside the element layer's thumbnail.

7. Open **Select > Inverse**, then press **DEL**, then **ESC**.

8. If the element layer has a Layer Style, press **ALT+click** and drag the **Layer Style** icon from the element layer to the decorative layer.

ADD A METALLIC FINISH

To add a metallic finish to an element:

1. Select the **Linear Gradient** tool, and from the options bar, open the **Gradient picker**.

2. Click the arrow button and select **Metals > Silver**.

3. Select the desired layer, and turn off other layers' visibility.

4. Lock the layer's transparent pixels.

5. Draw a gradient line from the upper left corner to the lower right corner. (If using a shape layer, simplify the layer when asked.)

6. Repeat Steps 3 – 5 for each layer that needs the metallic finish.

CREATE A MULTI-LAYER ELEMENT

To create a multi-layered element:

1. Create a new layer for each level of the element.

2. Fill each layer with a different color so you can see them as you build the element.

3. Lock the transparent pixels of each layer.

4. If desired, add a finish to each layer.

5. Select the base layer, open the **Artwork and Effects** palette (**Styles and Effects** palette in Photoshop Elements 4.0), open the **Bevels** gallery, and apply a bevel style.

6. Double-click the layer's **Styles** icon to adjust the bevel's size and distance.

7. Press **ALT+click** and drag the **Styles** icon from the base layer to the other layers.

8. Add a drop shadow below the base layer.

9. Save as a PNG file.

CREATE A DROP SHADOW FROM SCRATCH

To create a drop shadow from scratch:

1. Create a new layer named *shadow*, and position it below the element's layer.

2. Select the *shadow* layer, then press **CTRL** (**CMD** on a Mac) **+ click** inside the element's thumbnail.

3. Open **Edit > Fill Selection > Use: Black** and click **OK**.

4. Press **ESC** to turn off the selection marquee.

5. Select the shadow layer, then open **Filter > Blur > Gaussian Blur**.

6. Set the **Radius** to the desired size (example: 3 pixels).

7. Use the **Move** tool and **ARROW** keys to nudge the shadow a few spaces down and to the right.

8. If desired, change the *shadow* layer's opacity or color.

MODIFY A BRUSH PRESET

To modify an existing brush preset:

1. Select the **Brush** tool and from the options bar, open the **Brush Preset** palette.

2. Select or load a brush library.

3. Select a brush.

4. From the options bar, change the **Size**, **Mode**, or **Opacity**, or select the **Airbrush** feature.

5. Click **More Options** to change the brush's **Spacing**, **Hardness**, **Angle**, or **Roundness**.

6. Change the Foreground color to change the color a brush uses.

CREATE AND DEFINE A BRUSH

To create a new brush:

1. Open a blank file and create a drawing.

2. If you have a background layer, turn off its visibility.

3. Open **Edit > Define Brush**, give it a name and click **OK**.

To draw a dotted line:

1. Select a hard round brush.

2. Click **More Options** and change the **Spacing** option until you're satisfied. The higher the setting, the more space between "dots."

To use a photo as a brush:

1. Open the photo.

2. It it's too large, open **Image > Resize > Image Size** and reduce the width and height so that neither is larger than 2500 pixels.

3. Define the image as a brush.

SAVE AND LOAD A BRUSH LIBRARY

To save a new brush library:

1. Open **Edit > Preset Manager**. For **Preset Type**, select **Brushes**.

2. Select the brushes you want to save as a new library. (**SHIFT** or **CTRL+click** to select multiple brushes.)

3. Click **Save Set**, name the set, specify a location, and click **Done**.

To load a brush library from a CD or other source:

1. Save the library to the Photoshop Elements *Brushes* folder on your computer.

2. Quit Photoshop Elements and restart it. The new library will appear at the bottom of the list of libraries in the **Brushes** box. Select it.

3. If you save your library to a different folder, open the **Brush Preset** palette, click the arrow button, select **Load Brushes**, navigate to your library, and click **Load**.

To add a brush to an existing library:

1. Load the library.

2. Define a new brush. It appears in the **Brush Preset** palette.

3. From the **Brush Preset** palette, click the small arrow button and select **Save Brushes** (not **Save Brush**).

4. Select the library in which you created the new brush, then click **Save** to replace your library.

CONVERT A COLOR PHOTOGRAPH TO BLACK-AND-WHITE

To convert a color photo to grayscale mode:

1. Duplicate the photo layer, and turn off the original layer's visibility.

2. Select the duplicate layer, then open **Image > Mode > Grayscale**.

To desaturate a color photo to make a richer black-and-white image:

1. Open **Layer > New Adjustment Layer > Hue/Saturation**.

2. Check the **Group With Previous Layer** box, then click **OK**.

3. Drag the **Saturation** slider all the way to the left (-100).

4. Merge the photo layer and the *Hue/Saturation* layer (**SHIFT+click** the layers, then open **Layer > Merge Layers**).

DRAW AN EDGE EFFECT FOR A PHOTO

To draw an edge effect for a photo:

1. Use a marquee tool (**Rectangular**, **Ellipse**, or **Lasso**) to draw a selection marquee inside the margins of your photo.

2. Open **Select > Inverse**.

3. (Optional) To soften the edge, open **Select > Feather** and set the **Feather Radius** to **15 pixels** or higher.

4. Press **DEL** to remove the excess, then press **ESC** to turn off the marquee.

CREATE AND USE A MASK

To use a Photoshop Elements Crop Shape as a mask:

1. Select the **Custom Shape** tool. In the options bar, open the **Custom Shape Picker**.

2. Click the **Custom Shape Picker's** arrow button, click **Crop Shapes**, then select a Crop Shape.

3. With the crop shape layer selected, draw the Crop Shape mask just inside your photo's margins.

4. Press **CTRL** (**CMD** on a Mac) **+ click** the crop shape layer's thumbnail.

5. Select the photo layer and turn off visibility of the crop shape layer.

6. Open **Select > Inverse**.

7. (Optional) To soften the edge, open **Select > Feather** and set the **Feather Radius** to **15 pixels** or more.

8. Press **DEL**, then press **ESC** to turn off the marquee.

To create your own crop shape and use it as a mask:

1. Create a new layer named *mask shape*.

2. Fill the *mask shape* layer with black.

3. Select the **Eraser** tool, choose a brush tip, and erase the edges of the photo.

4. Press **CTRL** (**CMD** on a Mac) **+ click** the *mask shape* layer's thumbnail.

5. Select the photo layer and turn off visibility of the *mask shape* layer.

6. Open **Select > Inverse**.

7. (Optional) To soften the edge, open **Select > Feather** and set the **Feather Radius** to **15 pixels** or higher.

8. Press **DEL**, then press **ESC** to turn off the marquee.

9. (Optional) Save your new mask as a PNG file to use later. To use it again, open and copy it into your layout. Then repeat Steps 4 - 8.

USE A CLIPPING GROUP

To create a frame and mask for a Clipping Group:

1. Copy a photo into your layout. Resize as needed.

2. Add a new layer and name it *mask*.

3. Use a **Marquee** tool to draw a selection the shape you want the mask to be.

4. Fill the selection with black.

5. Move the *mask* layer below the photo layer.

6. Add a new layer and name it *frame*. Position this layer above the photo layer.

7. Use brushes (or any tool you like) to create a decorative frame for your photo.

8. To use the frame and mask, select the photo layer. Open **Layer > Group with Previous**.

9. To remove a Clipping Group, open **Layer > Ungroup**.

gallery

Scrapbookers are undoubtedly some of the most creative, talented, and inspiring people you could ever meet. And I've been so lucky to get to know so many of them!

I'd like you to meet five wonderful scrapbookers whose talents I admire. I invited each of them to use my designs in their own projects, which are showcased in this chapter. I know you'll be as excited by their results as I am!

ANNA ASPNES | ELMENDORF AFB, ALASKA

UK native, Alaska resident and fluent German speaker Anna Aspnes brings a global perspective to digital scrapbooking. Although she's a full-time mother to four-year-old Ella and two-year-old Luke, she makes time to design for both digital and paper scrapbooking companies. Much of Anna's work is featured on *designerdigitals.com*.

HOLLY MCCAIG | MANCHESTER, MISSOURI

Holly's formal design training shows through in her meticulous, technically proficient work. She takes special pride in designing and sharing her own digital kits and artistic elements at her Web site, *hollymccaigdesigns.com*.

KATE TEAGUE | DELTA, BRITISH COLUMBIA, CANADA

Kate likes to keep her pages fairly simple and clean-lined, although she's not afraid to try new techniques and step out of her comfort zone. Constantly learning and exploring new ways to do things, Kate is living up to her "scrap it like you mean it" mantra. For more about Kate go to *kate_teague.typepad.com*.

KRISTIE DAVID | HOUSTON, TEXAS

Kristie's bright, playful designs have earned her widespread recognition. As her alter ego "Shabby Princess," she sells her work online and as a Bo-Bunny Press branded line for those scrapbookers who can't give up their trimmers and adhesive. See Kristie's designs at *shabbyprincess.com* and *theshabbyshoppe.com*.

TIA BENNETT | PUYALLUP, WASHINGTON

Tia cried when her teacher told her she had to color inside the lines of the drawing on her worksheet. She'd just wanted to jazz up the page a little. To this day she is driven to challenge the ordinary. A much-published scrapbooker, Tia designs digital products, stamps and fonts and releases weekly designs at *designerdigitals.com*.

GALLERY

anna aspnes

144

kate teague

summer 2006

The older you get, the more fun you have with your cousins.

This past summer, the 5 of you had a blast playing together.

Swimming, bike riding, running, games, playing, you name it.

You are lucky to have so many cousins so close in age.

I love seeing you interacting with them and having so much fun!

cousin time

one handed camera shots

nothing like a few laughs and scrap talk

sofitel hotel, sanf francisco, nov. 2006

a visit that was short but

GK
grace kate

sweet

thanksgiving 2006

GOBBLE, GOBBLE

Mackenzie made this cute little hat at preschool. It was one of the first little projects that she brought home. She was so proud of her creation, wearing it all around the house saying, "Gobble, gobble, gobble." I have saved the little turkey in her school book, but I thought it was so cute, it deserved it's own layout. A little page to remember my little turkey by. Hee hee! And such a cute little turkey she was!

gobble, gobble, gobble

kristie david

tia bennett

a
family
affair

father

son

grand-daughter

daughter

it's pretty much
a given that there
will be an average
of 3 cameras at any
family gathering!

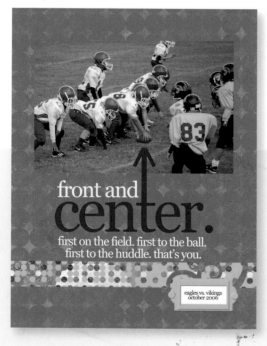

front and
center.
first on the field. first to the ball.
first to the huddle. that's you.

eagles vs. vikings
october 2006

braxton?
will you fly me?

fly boy

Hardly any convincing is necessary to get Jaden flying through Grandma & Grandpa's living room. Softest couch landing in the world! Braxton and Thomas took turns tossing him high and long. I remember doing this as a lad; makes me wish I still could! Oh, to be a lad again!